AF326706

THE
UNCONSCIOUS
BUYING
FORMULA

The Unconscious Buying Formula

How to Turn Neuroscience Into Trust, Sales, and Market Power

Alex Vonderhaar

Published by Game Changer Publishing

Paperback ISBN: 978-1-969372-78-0
Hardcover ISBN: 978-1-969372-80-3
Digital ISBN: 978-1-969372-81-0

www.GameChangerPublishing.com

To the unseen hand.
To the twitch before the thought,
the pupil's dilation before the word.

To the part of you that moves
before reason catches its breath—
the ancient pulse that still decides
what the modern mind pretends to choose.

I sing of the silent language beneath commerce,
of glances and gestures,
of patterns older than persuasion itself.

This is for the creators who see in the dark,
the marketers who would rather understand than manipulate,
the thinkers who study not the noise, but the nerve.

You who feel the world's heartbeat
beneath its headlines—
this book is for you.

For the fool who begins,
the magician who transforms,
the emperor who commands,
and the hermit who listens.

For every buyer who believes they decided freely—
and every seller humble enough to know they didn't.

I dedicate this to the mind beneath the mind.
The quiet genius inside all of us,
who buys, believes, and becomes—
long before we ever know why.

And most importantly, to my loving wife, Meghan, without you I would have
never made it. Thank you for the last decade we have shared together, and a
lifetime of adventures together.

Read This First

Just to say thanks for buying and reading my book, I would like to connect and give you your free resources!

Scan the QR Code Here:

THE UNCONSCIOUS BUYING FORMULA

HOW TO TURN NEUROSCIENCE INTO TRUST, SALES, AND MARKET POWER

ALEX VONDERHAAR

FOREWORD

By Taylor Welch

Most people think marketing is about getting "noticed."

But the real game is darker and far more expensive: you're not competing for attention, not anymore. You're competing, against every other business in the world, for nervous systems. In a world that is drowning in noise, the only brands that can win are the ones that make you feel before you think. Logic is often late to the party; the body decides first.

Safety, resonance, and emotional certainty—these are the new currencies.

People don't move or buy because it "makes sense." That used to be the case, but today there are too many competing messages, too many conflicting opinions, and too many signals. Our brains can't handle the load anymore. Our nervous systems cast the first vote, and the brain shows up with logic and timing, scrambling to justify decisions that have already been made without its Input.

Few people understand this like Alex. Even fewer can teach it with the level of proficiency and mastery that he provides in this book.

But don't be fooled: the book isn't just "more content."

It's ammunition for the future of your business; filled with real science and supportive frameworks for you to not only learn but to implement immediately in your organization. Most marketers are still stuck swinging hammers at the intellect. It isn't working; the loudest companies in the world today are burning out and wasting money while the aligned and nuanced architects of human emotion are scaling to record highs.

The masterpiece Alex has put together isn't just a random collection of hacks or tactics. It is an arsenal of weaponry that any company can use to understand their markets and their desires better. It is a blueprint for building belief, creating identity, and transmitting *real* signal so the right customers will lean in faster without needing to be pressured. Those who understand and master the contents of this book will no longer fight for attention; they will create it and command it.

Effortlessly.

You won't just make "more sales." Instead, you will create allegiance amongst buyers who don't just say "yes" one time—they stay, defend, refer, and build with you. When you understand how the mind and its various functions make buying decisions, you won't have to push people into deciding anything; you will simply allow them to experience alignment and coherence. When someone feels safe, they don't need persuasion; they only need permission.

Every chapter is packed with insights that I've spent many years and millions of advertising dollars learning the hard way. Alex is a genius who not only understands these principles but is passionate enough about them to give them to you for pennies on the dollar. If you implement them, I believe it will change not only your business, but also the way you operate in almost every facet of modern life.

The nervous system doesn't buy the words. It buys the frequency behind them. This isn't just about advertising and marketing—it applies to every sphere of influence you touch. Those who do not understand this are going to be fighting an uphill battle (and losing) for a long time.

Table of Contents

Outcome: **You'll stop blaming tools and tactics and start thinking like a strategist of the human mind, uncovering the invisible game every brand is actually playing.**

Outcome: **You'll master frameworks to decode unconscious motivators, collapse resistance, and speak directly to the brain's decision-making system.**

Outcome: You'll evolve from marketer to signal builder, becoming a force that shapes belief, earns trust at scale, and builds lasting market power.

INTRODUCTION

You've felt it, too, haven't you?

It usually starts with a whisper.

You're scrolling late at night, too tired to think, too wired to sleep.
Another ad. Another hack. Another coach promising to double your income in ninety days.
You don't click, but you feel the tug.
The colors. The tone. The way it *feels like it knows you.*

And just for a second… you wonder:
Why does this random piece of content understand me better than I understand myself?

You scroll again.
Another message.
Another ping.
Another perfectly crafted sentence that reaches through the glass and grabs your nervous system by the throat.

You tell yourself you're in control. That you're immune.
But a part of you, the part you can't explain, *moves anyway.*

This book is about that movement.
Not the logic of it.
The **feel** of it.
The unseen forces that shape belief before a word is spoken.
The emotional frequency that determines who we trust, who we buy from, and who we follow. Not because they asked, but because something in us said "yes" before we even knew why.

Most marketers have spent years learning tactics.
Click-through rates. Funnels. AI prompts.
But deep down, the real game was never about tools.
It was always about people.
About *behavior*.
About how the mind assigns meaning and how the nervous system decides what matters.

That's what this book unlocks.

The old game is dead.
We're no longer in an attention economy.
We're in a **nervous system war**.
And if you want to win, not by force but by resonance, you'll need a new map.

Here's the kicker... the information in this book transcends time, platform, and strategy because what you're about to learn is baked into deep psychological mechanisms, biases, and mental loopholes.

The Unconscious Buying Formula isn't just a book. It's a weapon.
It's a way to reshape belief, rewire behavior, and build trust so deeply that people will follow you without knowing why.

Not because you shouted the loudest, but because you became the clearest signal in a world full of noise.

I've spent the last decade studying influence, psychology, and building the United States' premier neuromarketing agency. I'm the manipulator and influencer behind you, maxing out credit cards and feeling good about it afterward.

You could consider this book a confession of my gnarliest methodologies or use it as a playbook to grow your own business. Or maybe you're just a psychology and marketing nerd like myself, and you want to learn some tips that have been battle-tested in hundreds of businesses.

Marketing and advertising are an expensive bloodbath when done wrong.

This book's primary goal is to equip all business owners, C-suite executives, and marketing and advertising professionals with the tools to thrive in the most rapidly advancing technological age we are likely to experience in our lifetime. I want you to win the war and take no prisoners in the process.

The nervous system war will continue as long as humans make purchases, and I'm beyond excited to see how you implement these tools to further your journey and business success.

Before we go any further, I need your permission.

This book will not simply teach you new tactics; it will install a new operating system.

If you're on board, here's what happens:

- The way you see influence will shift.
- The way you read persuasion will shift.
- The way you approach business growth, marketing, and advertising will shift.

You won't just be learning strategies.
You'll be rewiring instinct.

Most books give you tools. This one gives you triggers: psychological weapons designed to give you an unfair advantage in the modern marketplace, where the real war isn't for clicks but for nervous systems.

Once you see the world through this lens, you can't unsee it, and once you use it, you can't go back.

So, let me ask you… Are you ready for me to install?

Let's begin.

PART I
STEP INTO THE INVISIBLE GAME

CHAPTER 1

The Attention Economy Is Dead

Welcome to the Nervous System War

You don't buy cereal because of the copy.

You buy it because your hand moved before your brain did.

Same aisle. Same box. Same tiny hit of comfort.

The rational mind will tell you it made a choice.
But the truth?
The choice was made *for you* by the part of you that doesn't use language.

The subconscious.
The somatic.
The system that knows before you know.

This is the battlefield now.
Not logic.
Not persuasion.
But the **nervous system**.

And if you're still playing the "attention economy" game…
You've already lost.

The Lie You've Been Sold

Marketers have spent years worshiping at the altar of attention.

The tactics change—headlines, hooks, short-form loops—but the goal stays the same:

Get noticed.

Stay noticed.

Be remembered.

But here's the problem…

Attention isn't scarce anymore. Trust is.

That means your message is not competing with other brands.
It's competing with a body that doesn't want more input.

We live in an era of constant intrusion.
Every scroll. Every ping. Every ad.
A little theft of mental bandwidth.

And the brain's primary response?

Filter fast and disregard the consequences unless they are life-threatening.

Ignore what feels like work.
Ignore what feels like marketing.
Ignore what doesn't match the internal signal of safety, relevance, or identity.

Your headline isn't fighting other headlines.

It's fighting someone's **amygdala**, which has to decide if it should flee, freeze, or give you 0.3 seconds of focus.

You're Not Competing Against Other Brands—You're Competing Against Biology

Most marketing dies before it's even seen.

Not because it was bad, but because it *never made it through the filters that govern our conscious mind.*

The brain has layers of gatekeepers:

- The **reticular activating system** filters incoming data for relevance.
- The **default mode network** asks, "Is this about *me*?"
- The **amygdala** checks for threats.
- The **basal ganglia** run the same decision loops as yesterday and the day before that.

All of these gatekeepers are in the same group chat, forming a recurring bank of memories that guides us through daily decisions. On the surface, this is a great thing!

Cognitive neuroscientists estimate that we receive close to 11 million bits of information per second, but process only around 40 to 50 bits per second. This doesn't mean that we aren't receiving the information. Quite the opposite, we are only focused on what feels relevant, safe, or self-reinforcing.

If a message doesn't *feel* relevant, safe, or self-reinforcing within the first few seconds… it's already been kicked out of our mind before the logical side of our brain has the opportunity to evaluate if what you offer is truly valuable.

This is why "value-driven content" fails.
Because value is not the metric.
"Felt safety" is.

You could have the cure to someone's biggest pain…
But if it doesn't match the cadence of how their nervous system expects truth to sound, it gets deleted.

This is no longer about cognition.

This is about *recognition.*

The subconscious constantly scans for cues: tone, pacing, posture, frequency. If the signal matches the person's internal map, you get in. If it doesn't, you're just more noise.

This is why brilliant marketers fail to be intuitive ones. It's why great strategies flop and throwaway tweets go viral. The rules changed, and most people never noticed.

Attention That Clicks vs. Attention That Changes

You purchased this book for the honest truth, so grant me the opportunity to be blunt: not all attention is created equal.

There are two kinds of attention in this game:

1. Click Attention

It spikes. It disappears.
You get the view, the like, maybe the opt-in.
But it doesn't move anything meaningful.
No belief shift.
No identity resonance.
No sale.

It's the equivalent of honking your horn on the freeway during rush hour.
Everyone turns. Nobody does anything. You're forgotten.

You don't want eyeballs.
You want *embodiment*.

2. Embodied Attention

This is different.
This is when the body leans in, the reader inhales a bit deeper, and the words feel *too accurate* to ignore.

It's not louder.
It's deeper.

And once your message hits that level, you don't have to *sell* anymore.
You just have to keep speaking at that frequency.

You stop getting "customers."
You start getting believers.

You start to matter in a way that can't be measured by CPMs or click-through rates. Now they're not just listening. They're identifying with themselves through your brand.

This shift is often ignored by most marketers, business owners, and advertisers. Consequently, most businesses succumb to competitors who have this realization or have hired our agency to install this into their business.

The Real Economy Is Emotional Regulation

Relevance is emotional.

Trust is somatic.

What your audience really wants isn't more information.
It's **nervous system regulation**.

They're asking:

Can I relax into this message?
Does this person understand me better than I understand myself?
Will this make me feel more like who I believe I am?

This is why influence isn't loud. It's intimate.

Resonance doesn't come from shouting. It comes from **mirroring**.

A calm voice in a storm.
A familiar signal in chaos.
A word that names the emotion they haven't spoken yet.

That's what creates movement.

And the best part? It feels effortless.
Not to you. To *them.*

The nervous system recognizes something safe, familiar, or aspirational—and leans in.

We've left the world of funnel-builder marketing and entered the realm of neuromarketing.

Three Mental Shifts You Must Make Now

SHIFT 1: From Eyeballs to Nervous Systems

Forget views.

Ask, "What state of being is the person experiencing when this hits them?"

Anxious? Hopeful? Guarded? Skeptical?

Speak to the body, not just the brain.

SHIFT 2: From Capturing to Attuning

You're not a hunter.
You're a **tuning fork.**

When your message resonates with who they already believe they are (or who they're becoming), they move closer. Automatically.

Influence becomes effortless when attunement is high.

However, many business owners are afraid to smack that tuning fork against the table to find out what frequency actually resonates with their audience. It's like being blindfolded and randomly hitting keys on a piano until you find the right one. What a dumb way to approach client acquisition.

When you know the layout of a piano and how the keys function with the musical scales, you can tune into your audience's influence principles with ease.

SHIFT 3: From Persuasion to Permission

The deepest influence never feels like pressure.
It feels like **permission to trust.**

It's not "Let me convince you."
It's "Let me reflect back what you already feel but haven't found the words for yet."

Marketing that resonates gives people *language for what they already know to be true.*

When your message makes someone say, "That's it. That's exactly it," you've won.

If you've never had this experience on a sales call, social media post, or in your onboarding, then you are in the right place because something is out of alignment, and this book is going to get you sorted out.

Welcome to the War

This book isn't about grabbing attention.

It's about **earning access** to the subconscious, the somatic, and the self. This type of work requires a new set of tools.

Not tactics, but rather frameworks and models that are rooted in frequencies.

This is a way of understanding the emotional operating system your audience runs on and how to enter it without triggering defense mechanisms.

We're no longer marketers.

We are **signal builders**.

And if you can become the signal that regulates—not agitates—the nervous system of your market, you will win without saying a word.

If you've read this far, you already know the game you've been playing isn't the real one. The market doesn't respond to tools, hacks, or tactics— it responds to how well you understand the mind.

Most people will keep reading and take notes. A few will decide it's faster and smarter to have my team implement this work directly in their business. If that's you, here's your next step:

Schedule a private strategy call with my team. On this call, we'll look at your current marketing, show you where unconscious buying triggers are being missed, and map out how to install this formula in your business.

Don't just learn this—**live it**. Scan the QR code or click here to schedule your call: www.hiddenfallsmedia.com/contact

CHAPTER 2

Dopamine Dealers vs. Identity Architects

You've felt the high.

You post. You get a few likes. Maybe a comment. Maybe two. It spikes something in you. A little hit. A little charge. Then? It fades.

So, you chase it again.

New post. New angle. New headline. And again… and again…

This is how most brands operate: addicted to the reaction.
Built on borrowed dopamine.
Stuck in a loop where stimulus equals value and response equals success.

But if dopamine is the hit, identity is the *hook*. One of them scales. The other doesn't.

That's what this chapter is about:

- The difference between attention-driven marketing and identity-driven marketing
- Why dopamine fades but self-perception sticks
- And how to move from *dealer* to *architect* — from short-term spikes to long-term belief

The Real Addiction: Reaction-Based Marketing

Most content is written like crack. It's designed to get a hit, not to heal.

It's optimized for *what will spike the metric*—not what will shape the mind.

The result? Audiences become addicted to being entertained but resistant to being changed.

This is the trap because the algorithm trains you to chase spikes. The metrics reward it, and the dopamine reinforces it.

What you're left with in the end is that you don't have a brand. You have a casino. A slot machine. A message roulette with no narrative, no soul, and no stickiness.

True influence isn't reaction-based. It's reflection-based. It reflects something deeper to the reader. Something they already feel, believe, or aspire to become.

And once you start doing that, once your content stops being about *itself* and starts being about *them*, you stop being a Dopamine Dealer and start becoming an Identity Architect.

What Dopamine Marketing Gets Wrong

Dopamine marketing is external. It relies on:

- Novelty.
- Volume.
- Variable rewards.
- Short-term memory loops.

It's the "keep it coming" approach. Content as candy. You're not nourishing your audience, but you are numbing both yourself and them.

Here's the truth: The more dopamine you spike, the faster tolerance builds. The more content you pump, the more you have to escalate. Eventually, the shock fades, the surprise wears off, and the virality becomes noise.

This ultimately leaves you with a fatigued audience and a tired team.

Now, contrast that with *identity-based marketing...*

Identity-Based Marketing Is Built for Permanence

You know what people never get tired of? Themselves.

Who they are. Who they want to be. Who they fear they'll become.

If dopamine marketing hijacks behavior, identity marketing *aligns* with it. It doesn't just get a reaction. It makes the reader feel **seen**.

Seen = Safe.
Safe = Trusted.
Trusted = Bought.

Identity-based messages don't just entertain. They *mirror*. They don't just disrupt. They *anchor*.

You become part of their language. Their worldview. Their sense of self.

That's the deepest form of branding: when *your words become their thoughts.*

The Difference Between Dopamine and Identity

Most marketers are playing the dopamine game without realizing it. They're chasing reactions—likes, clicks, and fleeting attention—instead of building resonance, which is the foundation of lasting influence.

Let's break it down.

Dopamine Marketing

- **Disrupts pattern.** It interrupts your scroll but doesn't anchor to anything deeper.

- **Seeks reaction.** It's designed to spike your nervous system: *Wow, that was funny. That shocked me. I didn't see that coming.*

- **Is optimized for algorithms.** The goal is to trigger engagement signals that keep platforms happy.

- **Feels like entertainment.** It gives you a quick hit, but nothing sticks.

- **Requires volume.** You need to post daily, sometimes hourly, because the effect decays fast.

- **Creates followers.** But followers aren't buyers—they're spectators.

Identity Marketing

- **Disrupts patterns.** Not just another clickbait or "scroll-stopper", but instead locks into something deeper within their soma.

- **Seeks resonance.** It isn't about reaction; it's about recognition: *That's me. That's who I want to be.*

- **Is optimized for alignment.** Instead of chasing the algorithm, it reinforces your customer's self-image.

- **Reinforces patterns.** It validates the way people see themselves and anchors your product inside their story.

- **Feels like insight.** Not entertainment, but revelation—a piece of truth they can't unsee.

- **Requires accuracy.** You don't need to post ten times a day. One precise message can land harder than a hundred throwaways.

- **Creates advocates.** Customers don't just buy from you; they defend you, promote you, and build with you.

This is why you can have **100,000 followers and zero sales**, because all you did was stimulate without creating stickiness. Meanwhile, someone with one-tenth of that following is moving millions because they're **architecting belief**, not chasing attention.

You don't need hundreds of thousands of followers to be influential. In fact, as of 2025, most social media algorithms have tilted back in favor of *relevance over reach*. The machines are no longer rewarding sheer scale; they're rewarding how deeply your content connects to the **user's identity**.

That's a huge win for you because it means you don't need to compete with massive accounts pumping out endless content. You can design messages that **mirror your customer's self-image**, content that reinforces who they already believe themselves to be inside the story your brand is telling.

That's the shift: **from dopamine to identity, from clicks to conviction, from followers to believers.**

The Architect's Advantage

The Identity Architect doesn't need to flood the feed. They don't need to hack the algorithm.
They just need to wire themselves into the *emotional logic* of their audience.

When a message aligns with identity, it bypasses resistance.
It doesn't feel like persuasion. It feels like recognition.

Here's how they do it:

1 **Reinforce Aspiration (Who I Want to Be Seen As)**
   - Every human carries a future self-image: fitter, wealthier, more respected, freer.
   - Identity Architects echo this aspiration back, not as a fantasy but as if it's already true.
   - The message doesn't say, *You could be this.* It whispers, *This is already you. Let me show you the proof.*
   - That reinforcement creates *momentum* because people will always move toward the identity that feels most congruent.

2 **Challenge Fear (Who I Never Want to Become)**
   - Identity isn't just about who we're becoming. It's about what we're running from.
   - The best messages remind the audience of what's at stake: irrelevance, failure, regret, mediocrity.
   - The architect doesn't hammer pain points—they frame identity threats.

- o Example: "If you're not building resonance, you're building noise. And noise is forgotten."

3 Validate Secrets (What I Believe but Never Say Out Loud)
- o Everyone carries unspoken truths—things they *feel* deeply but don't articulate.
- o Identity Architects mines those hidden beliefs and gives them language.
- o When your audience reads your words and thinks, *Finally, someone said it,* you've locked into their nervous system. That's when you become their translator of reality.

The Dopamine Dealer's Goal: Be noticed.
The Identity Architect's Goal: Be *remembered.*

That's the distinction.
Dopamine Dealers chase virality.
Identity Architects go visceral.

They aren't asking, "How wide can this spread?"
They're asking, "How deep can this stick?"

When it sticks, something magical happens:

- Your words become their inner monologue.
- Your brand becomes shorthand for their belief system.
- They don't just consume you. They *carry you.*

That's the architect's advantage: permanence.
While dealers fight for clicks, architects build culture.

The Question You Must Answer

Every message you publish, every post you write, every headline you test must run through one brutal filter:

Am I rewarding someone's nervous system or reshaping their self-image?

If it's the former, expect churn.

Short-term spikes. Followers today, gone tomorrow. A cycle of endless feeding with nothing to show for it but exhaustion.

If it's the latter, expect compounding returns.

Because identity compounds.

Trust compounds.

Every word that reinforces who someone *is* or who they're becoming lays down another brick in the architecture of allegiance.

We need to rewire the truth:

- **Dopamine content disappears when the scroll ends.**
- **Identity content lingers when the phone shuts off.**

One gets forgotten in minutes.

The other reshapes someone's internal map and echoes for years.

And when you do that long enough, for enough people…

You stop being a brand.

You become a mirror.

The reflection people turn to when they need to remember who they are.

This is the architect's path.

It doesn't promise easy hits. It promises lasting power.

In the next chapter, we'll go deeper into the neurological reasons **why logic fails and frequency wins.**

But for now, burn this into your mind:

Dopamine creates addiction.

Identity creates allegiance.

And only one of them will survive when the algorithm moves on.

CHAPTER 3

Why Logic Fails and Frequency Wins

You've seen it happen.

You present the perfect offer. Flawless logic. Obvious value. Maybe even a limited-time bonus.

And still, no sale.

Not because the information was wrong, but because the *signal* was off.

This is one of the most misunderstood truths in persuasion: people don't act because something makes sense. They act because something feels coherent at the level of the nervous system.

Before the brain ever decodes a word, the body is scanning for safety, congruence, and trust. If the signal feels off, the logic never even gets a chance.

That's why logic is the weakest form of persuasion. Not because facts don't matter, but because facts only matter once the nervous system has already said "yes."

This chapter will show you why most arguments fail, why frequency beats formulas, and how resonance operates less like "woo" and more like *biology.*

The Great Persuasion Lie

You were taught to believe in the power of a good argument.
That if you lined up your facts, made your case airtight, and presented your evidence clearly, you'd win.

Humans are not rational creatures who occasionally feel.
We are emotional creatures who occasionally justify.

When logic and emotion go to war, emotion wins. Every. Single. Time.

Think about it:

- People don't buy luxury watches because they "tell time better." They buy them because of what it *feels like* to wear one.

- People don't choose presidents based on policy white papers. They choose the candidate who *feels like* safety, strength, or change.

- People don't stay loyal to brands because of rational comparisons. They stay loyal because the brand *mirrors who they believe they are.*

The problem isn't logic itself. It's when you use it.

Logic works after belief has taken root. Not before.
It cements. It rationalizes. It justifies.

Try to use logic to *build* belief? You're dead in the water.
Use logic to *support* a belief already formed? Now it works like rocket fuel.

This is why your perfectly crafted argument falls flat while someone else's vague, emotionally charged pitch dominates.

It's not about clarity. It's about *coherence.*

Clarity is how well your argument makes sense on paper.
Coherence is how well your message harmonizes with the emotional frequency already vibrating inside your audience.

People don't ask, "Is this argument valid?"
They ask, "Does this feel like me? Does this feel like truth?"
And once the answer is yes, logic can finally come in as the supporting actor, not the lead.

Here's the piece most marketers never grasp: persuasion doesn't begin in the mind. It begins in the body.

This is why logic-first persuasion fails so often. It assumes people are listening to your words. They're not. At least, not at first.

Before a sentence makes it to the rational brain, it has to clear the body's security system. The nervous system is like a bouncer at the club of consciousness. It decides what gets in and what gets bounced.

And what's it scanning for? Not facts. Not clarity. But *frequency.*

Is this message safe?
Does this tone feel aligned?
Does this signal match what I already believe about myself?

If the vibe feels off, the nervous system slams the door before the words even register. The most logical argument in the world dies on the sidewalk, not because it lacked merit, but because it lacked resonance.

This is why we're so easily swayed by a charismatic speaker with half-baked points and so resistant to the nervous, over-prepared professional with flawless logic. One feels congruent; the other feels wrong.

Here's the sequence most people never map:

1. **Vibe hits first.** Pacing, tone, energy—they fire the nervous system's threat/relevance detectors.

2. **Emotion follows.** Safety or suspicion, resonance or rejection.

3. **Logic lags.** Only once the signal feels coherent does the rational brain engage to justify what the body has already decided.

Most are guilty of inverting the sequence, which means that if you lead with logic instead of vibe, you're asking the brain to override the body. And the body almost never loses.

That's why clarity isn't enough. You can line up your arguments like soldiers, but if they march in at the wrong frequency, the gates never open.

This means that the first job of influence isn't to be right. It's to be received.

Get the nervous system on your side, and logic can follow as reinforcement. Ignore the nervous system, and logic never gets its turn.

That's the bridge most marketers miss. Persuasion is not words → then feelings. It's vibe → then emotion → then words.

And once you understand that sequence, the rules of the game change forever.

The Nervous System Doesn't Speak English

Before the brain decodes a word, the body decodes a vibe.

Pacing. Tone. Syntax. Breath. Emotional charge.
These land first, and they decide whether the words that follow will be received as truth, ignored as noise, or rejected as a threat.

Here's why:

- The amygdala fires before the prefrontal cortex has time to "think."
- The nervous system scans for *safety* before the brain processes for *sense.*
- And if the body says *unsafe* or *incongruent,* the words never even make it to conscious evaluation.

This means that your message isn't judged on content. It's judged on *coherence.* On whether the signal *feels* aligned before it's even translated into language.

Think of your message like a radio signal.
If the frequency is off, the words get distorted.
Static. Mistrust. Discomfort.
But when the tuning is precise, the message comes through clean. It's effortless, obvious, and undeniable.

What I have found throughout hundreds of companies is that most people speak at the wrong frequency.
They sound anxious, desperate, performative, or misaligned with their own message.
So, even if their content is brilliant, the delivery collapses it.

Why? Because the nervous system whispers, *Nope. Doesn't feel right.*

This is why a beginner with the right frequency can outperform a seasoned pro with the wrong one.

The audience isn't evaluating your resume, credentials, or perfectly polished pitch.

They're evaluating your **resonance.**

The question isn't "Do these words make sense?"
The question is "Do these words feel safe, aligned, and true in my body?"

Get that right, and the nervous system opens the door.
Get it wrong, and it slams shut before the brain ever reads the copy.

We just established that the nervous system doesn't speak English.
It speaks in tone, pacing, and vibe. It listens for coherence before it listens for content.

And this is where most marketers crash. They memorize formulas. They copy frameworks. They repeat word-for-word scripts that worked for someone else, but then they are left to wonder why the same words fall flat when they say them or use them in your campaigns.

It's not the words that are broken. It's the frequency carrying them.

If your signal feels anxious, desperate, or misaligned, no formula can save you. The body has already said "no."

Which brings us to the truth most pros don't want to hear…

Frequency > Formula

The dirty secret of marketing is this: most formulas work.
Headlines. Frameworks. Closing scripts.
They've been tested, proven, and optimized.

I call these types of marketers "button-pushers." It's not that they aren't educated in how things work together, but they are stuck memorizing formulas. The problem with memorizing formulas is that they only work when they ride the right frequency.

Frameworks, formulas, and battle-tested methodologies are just the table stakes. If you wanna play the game, you gotta know the rules.

You've seen this play out in your own business at some point. You buy a funnel course or just rip off and duplicate someone else's funnel (no judgment, we've all done it), only to have the results come up completely flat. The same words that made one person millions can make another look like a fraud.

This happens because the nervous system isn't evaluating the syntax. It's evaluating the signal underneath.

If your internal state is desperate, the formula will broadcast desperation.
If your state is anxious, the formula will amplify anxiety.
If your state is congruent, the formula will sound like truth.

That's why the beginner with resonance outperforms the veteran with scripts.
It's not about getting the lines right.
It's about getting the vibe right.

Frequency is the invisible language of trust.
It's what tells your audience:

- *I believe this person believes in themselves.*
- *I feel safe here.*
- *I can relax into this message.*

And once those gates open, the words can finally do their work.

But if the frequency is off?
The gate never opens.
And no amount of clever copy will force its way through.

Formulas create structure.
Frequency creates belief.
And belief is the only thing that compounds.

So, stop asking, "What's the right script?"
Start asking, "What signal am I sending when I say it?"

At the end of the day, the nervous system doesn't buy the words.
It buys the **frequency behind them.**

We must move from frequency to resonance if we are going to create ROI in our marketing and advertising.

So, here's the paradox:
Formulas aren't useless. They're just incomplete.

Frequency is the entry point, but it's not the entire architecture.

Think of it like building a house.
Frequency is the foundation. If it's crooked, nothing else will stand.
But once it's stable, you still need walls, framing, and a roof.

The same is true in persuasion.
Frequency gets you through the door.
Resonance keeps you in the room.
And logic, when it finally arrives, gives people permission to stay.

This is where most marketers fail.

They obsess over the top layer of the testimonials, the proof, the bullet points, while completely ignoring the ground their message is built on.

If you want to consistently land, if you want your words to bypass resistance and stick to memory, you need all three layers working together.

Let's break them down.

The Three Layers of Resonant Messaging

Every message that lands follows the same law: it moves through the nervous system in layers.
Miss a layer, and persuasion fails before it begins.

Think of it like a security checkpoint. Three gates. Each one must be cleared before the next opens.

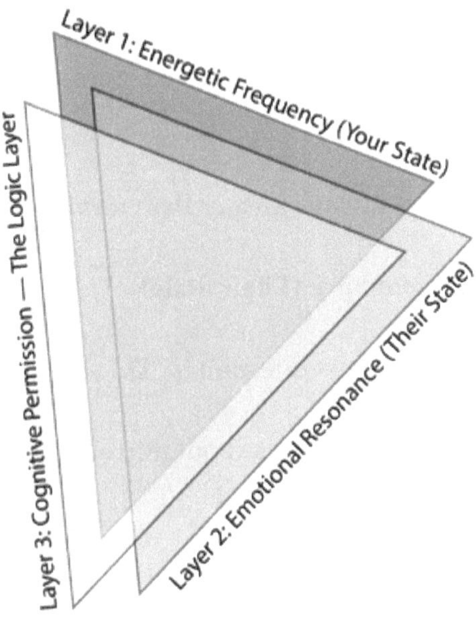

Layer 1: Energetic Frequency (Your State)

This is the *pre-language signal.* It's not what you say; it's what your body broadcasts before the words arrive.

- Calm vs. frantic.
- Certain vs. doubtful.
- Congruent vs. performative.

Your frequency is the first thing the audience receives. It tells their nervous system in microseconds:

- *Am I safe with this person?*
- *Do they believe themselves?*
- *Can I trust the signal underneath the words?*

If the body says "no," the message never reaches the brain. The gate slams shut.

You can hand two people the same sales script. One radiates calm certainty; the other radiates desperate need. Same words. One converts; the other repels.

This is why frequency is always greater than formula.

Layer 2: Emotional Resonance (Their State)

Once the gate is open, the next question is "Do you understand me?"

This isn't about clever phrasing. It's about mirroring the emotional reality your audience is already living.

When you name the hidden emotion (fear, hope, anxiety, desire), people feel seen.

And "seen" equals "safe."
Safety creates trust.

Nike doesn't sell shoes by talking about materials. They sell the emotion of victory, grit, and defiance. Apple doesn't sell circuits. They sell creativity and belonging.

Skip this layer, and your words might be correct, but they'll feel hollow. The audience nods politely, but they don't move.

Layer 3: Cognitive Permission (The Logic Layer)

Logic is the final gate. The role of logic is not to *create* belief but to *reinforce* it once the body has already said "yes."

- Proof
- Testimonials
- Case studies
- Numbers

These don't persuade on their own. They give the mind permission to agree with what the nervous system has already decided.

That's why stacking facts at the beginning of your pitch fails. If the gate hasn't been opened, the opportunity can't get through.

Think about politics for a second…
Nobody switches sides because of a white paper. Policy is the last gate, not the first.

Donald Trump understood this better than anyone.

In 2016, he didn't win because of detailed policy arguments. He won because his *frequency* cut through the noise.

- While career politicians sounded polished and rehearsed, Trump's tone was raw, unpredictable, and emotionally charged.

- Love him or hate him, his energy came across as *unfiltered*. And in an era of deep distrust, that frequency was perceived as "real" by millions of voters.

Once the nervous system says, *This person feels real,* the door is open.

Then came the resonance. Trump didn't start with data points; rather, he started with *identity anchors.*

- "Make America Great Again" wasn't a policy. It was a mirror. It spoke directly to a felt sense of loss, pride, and belonging.

- He named the emotions many Americans were already carrying but felt nobody in power was reflecting back to them: frustration, anger, fear of decline, hope for restoration.

That's resonance. He made people feel seen by holding up the mirror of the current situation to them while saying through his various messages, "I see you," "I understand why you're upset, and I'm upset, too," "What has happened is not fair to you."

Only after that emotional connection was built did policy or logic have a chance to matter.

- The wall
- Trade deals
- Jobs returning to America

These were never airtight arguments. On their own, they might not have been persuasive at all, but once belief was established, logic served as *reinforcement.*

It gave voters permission to defend the decision they'd already made emotionally.

Fast forward to 2024: the pattern repeated. While opponents buried voters in detailed plans, Trump doubled down on frequency and resonance. The cadence of his speech, the nicknames, the rallies are all designed to *bypass logic* and tune directly into the nervous system of his audience.

Critics dismissed it as shallow. But they missed the sequence and clearly didn't understand the rules of persuasion.

- Frequency got attention.
- Resonance created identity alignment.
- Logic, even shaky logic, became believable because the first two gates were already open.

This is why half the country heard incoherence while the other half heard conviction. They weren't listening to the same words. They were tuned to different frequencies.

And that's the lesson in politics, business, marketing, and everything else in life: logic doesn't lead; it follows.

Most brands start at Layer 3. They bury their audience under data, proof, and bullet points. Then they wonder why conversion stays flat.

They ignored the sequence!

1. **Energy first.** If your frequency is off, no one listens.
2. **Emotion second.** If you don't resonate, no one cares.
3. **Logic last.** Once the gates are open, logic seals the deal.

This is the foundation for everything else in this book.

Get the layers right, and every framework, funnel, and campaign you run will work harder.

Get them wrong, and nothing else matters.

Frequency Isn't Woo—It's the Physics of Trust

Let's clear something up right away:

When I talk about "frequency," I'm not asking you to buy crystals or hum in a circle.

Frequency is not vibe. It's not mood. It's not positive thinking.

It's the professional application of **signal coherence**: the alignment between what you believe internally and what you broadcast externally.

The human nervous system is exquisitely tuned to detect alignment within a few feet of another person. Research shows that our bodies pick up cues of safety, congruence, and threat within a radius of **five to eight feet**, often before a word is spoken. This isn't mysticism. It's biology. Our nervous systems are designed to entrain with each other.

Your tone, heart rate, and posture all broadcast a signal, and people feel it.

That's why you can walk into a room and instantly know who's calm, who's frantic, and who's faking it.

Think about the last time you heard a leader speak. Within seconds, you probably felt whether you trusted them, not because of the facts they presented, but because of *how* they carried themselves.

- Was their tone steady or shaky?

- Did their words match their body language?
- Did you sense conviction or performance?

That's frequency. Not in the "woo-woo" sense. In the neurological sense.

The nervous system picks up micro-signals faster than language: pacing, tone, posture, cadence. Before the rational mind has decoded a single word, the body has already made its decision: safe or unsafe, congruent or incongruent, trust or doubt.

This is why frequency matters. It's not about energy as a mood... It's about trust as a transmission.

So, how do you make this practical?

Before you hit publish on a post, deliver a pitch, or walk into a meeting, ask yourself these questions:

1. *Am I regulated or reactive?*
   If you're in fight-or-flight mode, your nervous system broadcasts it. Your tone sharpens, your pacing speeds up, your words tighten. Audiences may not consciously know what's wrong, but they'll feel the signal: *This person is unsettled. Don't trust them.*

2. *Am I speaking from truth or from tension?*
   When you speak from tension (trying to prove, trying to impress, trying to defend), the audience feels the performance. When you speak from truth (aligned belief, lived experience, congruence), the audience feels a sense of safety.

3. *Does this message feel like a performance or a pattern interrupt rooted in clarity?*
   Performance feels rehearsed and brittle. Clarity feels grounded and confident. One triggers resistance; the other earns permission.

Frequency tuning doesn't mean "calm down." It means regulate first, speak second. Because resonance follows regulation. People don't remember what you said. They remember how your *signal* made them feel.

Why Frequency Outweighs Formulas

Frequency isn't abstract. It has **direct commercial consequences.**

- A salesperson with a shaky tone can tank a proven script.
- A marketer who feels desperate can ruin a perfect funnel.
- A leader who signals doubt can collapse team confidence even when the strategy is sound.

The reverse is also true:

- A regulated founder with average slides can raise millions.
- A marketer with congruence in their words can outperform "optimized copy."
- A calm, aligned signal can close clients before the contract is even read.

That's because **trust isn't claimed. It's felt.** And frequency is the nervous system's shorthand for trust.

Frequency Creates Conversion

When what you *believe,* what you *say,* and what you *signal* all align, you become magnetic.

The audience doesn't just hear your words. They feel the integrity behind them. They think, *This person believes themselves.* And that coherence is what collapses resistance.

But when your frequency is off, when you're saying things you don't fully believe, exaggerating results, or performing with confidence you don't have, the nervous system catches it instantly.

Even if people can't articulate why, they hesitate. They scroll past. They hold back their credit card.

That's the difference between short-term attention and long-term allegiance.

In the end, **frequency isn't about looking polished. It's about being congruent.**
And congruence is the currency of trust.

The Core Lesson

People won't remember every word you said. They won't replay your bullet points or memorize your slides.

But they will remember how your signal made them feel.

That's the professional power of frequency: it's not a vibe. It's a weapon—and the fastest path to becoming felt, trusted, and chosen in a marketplace flooded with noise.

You don't win with logic. You win with **coherence.**

Message matches motive. Motive matches energy. Energy matches the moment.

When those three align, people move.

Frequency isn't a hack. It's the *truth beneath the tactic,* and when the nervous system recognizes that truth, it says the only word that matters: **"yes."**

CHAPTER 4

Belief Is the Real Conversion Metric

Nobody buys a product. Nobody buys a service.

What they really buy is a **belief upgrade.**

- Belief about themselves.
- Belief about what's possible.
- Belief about how the world works and their role in it.

Think about it:

- Nobody buys a gym membership just to access weights. They buy the belief that *I can change my body.*

- Nobody buys life insurance because they like paperwork. They buy the belief that *my family will be safe when I'm gone.*

- Nobody buys an iPhone because they need another rectangle in their pocket. They buy the belief that *I am the kind of person who belongs on the cutting edge.*

Every transaction is an identity transaction. Every sale is a story of transformation.

And this is the part most marketers miss: people don't say "yes" because of what they're *getting*. They say "yes" because of what saying "yes" allows them to *believe*.

That's why the best salespeople and the best brands don't push offers; they engineer belief transfer.

Once you understand this, the game changes. You stop selling features and start shaping reality.

The Belief Stack

Every human decision runs through a sequence of subconscious filters.
Ignore them, and your conversion stalls.
Stack them, and resistance collapses.

This is the **real sales funnel.** Not stages, software, or automations, but the invisible gauntlet every nervous system runs before it says "yes."

1. Do I believe this person gets me?

This is the empathy filter. Before anyone cares about your product, they need to feel seen.

- If the message sounds generic, you fail.
- If it mirrors their inner world, you pass.

When Peloton first scaled, they weren't selling bikes. They were saying, "We understand the guilt of missing workouts, the desire for community, the pride of pushing yourself." They weren't selling exercise; they were saying, "We get you."

Fail here, and the funnel ends. Nothing else matters if they don't believe that you understand their world.

2. Do I believe they're telling the truth?

This is the congruence filter. People don't just listen to your words; they scan your tone, delivery, and track record.

- Do you actually believe what you're saying?
- Do your results match your promises?
- Does the way you show up feel aligned?

This is why Warren Buffett's plain, no-BS communication style creates instant trust. He doesn't sound like he's selling. He sounds like he's stating reality. His delivery signals truth.

If you wobble here, if your frequency feels off, even the most polished case study won't save you.

3. Do I believe this will work for me?

This is the relevance filter. Even if they believe you, they're still asking, "But will it work in my situation?"

- General proof isn't enough.
- They need *mirrored proof*: stories, case studies, and testimonials that look like them.

Weight-loss programs fail when they show perfect before-and-after models. They succeed when they show *real people* who look, live, and struggle like the prospect and then overcome their weight problem.

Your job isn't to convince people that the system works in theory. It's to prove that it can work *for people like them.*

4. Do I believe I'm the kind of person who follows through?

This is the identity filter, aka the final gate.

Even if they trust you and believe what you're offering will work for people like them, they'll still hesitate if they don't believe *they* can follow through.

- This is why great marketing doesn't just sell a product. It sells identity.

- It says, "You are the kind of person who does this. You are the kind of person who finishes. You are the kind of person who belongs here."

Nike doesn't just sell shoes. "Just Do It" is an identity installation. It tells the customer, "You are the kind of person who shows up, who doesn't quit, who keeps moving."

When you help someone see themselves differently, conversion becomes inevitable.

Forget stages, software, or clever hacks.

The real funnel is belief stacking:

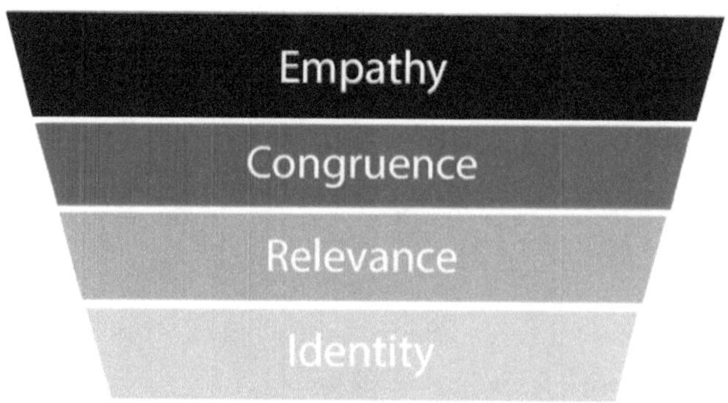

1. **Do you get me?** (Empathy)
2. **Do I trust you?** (Congruence)
3. **Will this work for me?** (Relevance)
4. **Am I the kind of person who does this?** (Identity)

If belief doesn't stack, conversion doesn't happen.

But when it does, you're no longer selling. You're leading someone into a new version of themselves.

This cannot be done once and forgotten. It is an endless cycle that needs to be repeated until your audience mirrors all of this back to you. Many quit this process way too soon. This process needs to be baked into every phase of your customer journey.

If done correctly, your lifetime value will soar, your customer acquisition cost will drop, and your churn rate will become tolerable.

Information Doesn't Convert—Interpretation Does

Most marketers operate like teachers. They dump information.
Data. Benefits. Features… And then they wonder why nobody moves.

However, people don't act on information. They act on **interpretation.**

The human brain isn't built to respond to raw facts. It's built to respond to *meaning*. Every number, every stat, every feature has to run through a filter:

- *What does this mean about me?*
- *What does this prove about my place in the world?*
- *What does this validate that I already suspected?*

If the fact doesn't answer one of those questions, it gets discarded. Fast.

Neuroscience is clear: the rational brain (neocortex) is rarely in the driver's seat of decision-making. The emotional brain (limbic system) makes the call, and then the rational brain comes in afterward to justify it.

That's why "educating your market" is a dangerous myth. You can bury a prospect in charts, graphs, and proof, and still lose them.

Not because the data is wrong, but because it wasn't *framed.* Information without interpretation is just noise.

Interpretation is **story or meaning applied to fact**.
It's not about what the fact *is*. It's about what the fact *means*.

- **The fact:** "These shoes are made with carbon-neutral materials."

- **The interpretation:** "When you buy these, you're the kind of person who protects the planet."

- **The fact:** "This car goes 0–60 in 3.5 seconds."

- **The interpretation:** "When you drive this, you're powerful, dominant, untouchable."

- **The fact:** "This program has helped a thousand people lose weight."

- **The interpretation:** "People just like you finally took control, and so can you."

The shift is subtle, but it's everything. Facts inform. Interpretation transforms.

Apple is the master at this. If you pay attention to their website, marketing, and ads, you'll notice that they don't sell megapixels, gigabytes, or processors. They sell identity. Their interpretation of the facts is "This isn't a phone. It's a piece of who you are."

Tesla doesn't sell electric cars with technical specs. They sell disruption. They sell a belief: "Owning this car means you're part of the future, not stuck in the past."

Politics works the same way. Policy papers rarely move the needle. However, when a candidate frames those policies in terms of what they *mean for the voter's identity* (safety, power, belonging), belief shifts.

Before you share a piece of data, ask yourself:

1. *What does this fact mean about them?*
   a. *Does it reinforce who they want to be?*
   b. *Does it validate what they already feel?*

2. *What story does this fact live inside?*
   a. *Is it part of a bigger emotional narrative?*
   b. *Or is it just floating in isolation?*

3. *What identity does this fact confirm?*
   a. *Does it make them feel smarter, safer, stronger, more aligned?*

You don't need more facts. You need to shape what the facts mean.

Because logic makes people think.
Interpretation makes people move.

Once you learn to shift from *teacher* to *translator of meaning*, you'll never look at a sales page, ad, or speech the same way again.

Belief—Emotional Logic

John Mayer once wrote:

"Is there anyone who
Ever remembers changing their mind from
The paint on a sign?
Is there anyone who really recalls
Ever breaking rank at all
For something someone yelled real loud one time?"

Belief doesn't bend easily. Once it takes root, it resists logic, arguments, and even evidence.

As Mayer puts it later, *"Belief is a beautiful armor, but makes for the heaviest sword."*

That's the paradox, isn't it? Belief protects us, but it also traps us. It shields our sense of self while locking us into patterns we rarely escape.

And this is the key lesson most marketers never learn:

Logic makes people think.
Belief makes people move.

Belief is nothing more than **emotional logic**: a story that explains the world in a way that *feels true*.

Emotional logic is how the brain creates shortcuts.

- The rational brain takes time to process data.
- The emotional brain moves faster, spotting patterns and assigning meaning almost instantly.

That meaning *feels* like logic, but it's logic built on emotion, not evidence.

Example: "If I work hard, I'll succeed."
That's not a mathematical proof. It's an emotional story, but it feels like logic to the person who holds it.

The nervous system doesn't ask, *Is this objectively true?* It asks, *Does this story reduce uncertainty and make me feel safe?*

That's why emotional logic is so powerful. It creates a coherent story, and once people have a coherent story, they'll fight to defend it, even against contradictory facts.

Most businesses try to win by offering *better solutions.*

- Faster
- Cheaper
- Smarter

But people don't actually want the best solution. They want the best **story**.

- Airbnb isn't "a website to rent someone's spare bedroom." It's "belong anywhere."
- CrossFit isn't "a workout program." It's "a tribe of warriors training together."
- A Rolex isn't "a timepiece." It's "proof of success."

The solution is secondary. The story is primary because it explains what the solution *means.*

This is what most marketers miss. They pile on proof, thinking more data equals more persuasion. But proof is only persuasive when it fits inside a pattern the audience already recognizes.

If the pattern doesn't exist, the proof bounces.

That's why conspiracy theories spread so easily, not because they're more factual, but because they're more coherent stories. They provide people with a framework that feels emotionally logical, and once that pattern is established, every new fact is bent to fit it.

In marketing, the same rule applies. Your audience isn't asking, "Is this technically true?" They're asking, "Does this fit the pattern of how I already see myself and the world?"

If the answer is "yes", resistance collapses.

Your job isn't to make the offer make sense.
Your job is to make the story of saying "yes" feel obvious.

- A "yes" should feel like completing a sentence they've been writing in their head.
- A "yes" should feel like a puzzle piece clicking into place.
- A "yes" should feel like, *Of course. This is who I am. This is what I do.*

That's emotional logic. And once you learn how to build it, you stop trying to out-argue competitors and start out-believing them.

People don't want better solutions.
They want better stories.

They don't need proof.
They need a pattern they recognize.

Belief is emotional logic.
And emotional logic is the real engine of conversion.

The Belief Transfer Effect

Every high-converting brand, campaign, or salesperson operates off one principle:

You cannot install behavior without first transferring belief.

This is why some sales pages convert even when they're ugly, why some emails hit even when they break all the copywriting rules, and why certain leaders move people without needing slides, scripts, or polish.

Because the **frequency of belief** is higher than the **structure of persuasion.**

If the person writing the words, recording the video, or standing on the stage *truly believes* in the outcome, the audience can feel it. And if they don't? The audience can sense the wobble.

Human beings are wired for congruence detection. Long before the rational brain processes arguments, the nervous system scans for alignment:

- Does this person *believe* what they're saying?
- Do their tone, body language, and words match?
- Do they radiate conviction, or do they leak doubt?

This is why mirror neuron research matters: our brains are designed to *catch states* from others. Belief is contagious. Doubt is, too, and this is why so many pitches collapse. It's not that the copy was bad. It's that the messenger didn't believe it enough to transmit conviction.

You've felt this before.

A founder talks about their company with fire in their voice. They stumble over words, and their slides are average, but you *believe them.*

Contrast that with the polished salesperson delivering a perfect pitch deck, hitting every scripted line… yet you walk away unconvinced. The difference isn't tactics. It's transmission.

Belief isn't something you write. It's something you transfer.

Brands That Transfer Belief

- **Tesla**: Elon Musk often rambles, stumbles, and derails mid-presentation. However, he radiates belief in the mission, and investors, customers, and fans catch it. The words are secondary. The transmission is primary.

- **Nike**: "Just Do It" wasn't persuasive because of clever copy. It was persuasive because it carried the company's core belief: that every human being is an athlete. Customers didn't just buy shoes. They caught the belief.

- **Politics:** Trump (2016, 2024) and Obama (2008) operated on opposite ends of the spectrum, but both won the same way. They transmitted belief in their vision. Their audiences caught the conviction first, then rationalized it later.

You can't fake belief. The nervous system will catch the lie. But you can build it, anchor it, and broadcast it.

1. **Start with yourself.**
    - Do you *truly* believe in your offer?
    - If not, what's missing? Proof? Experience? Conviction?
    - Until you believe, your audience won't.

2 Collapse internal doubt.
- o Any tension or uncertainty leaks out.
- o Resolve objections in yourself before you try to resolve them for others.

3 Transmit through state.
- o Speak, write, and create from regulation.
- o Belief carries strongest when your nervous system is calm, congruent, and convicted.

Belief always precedes behavior. You cannot install a new action in your market (buy, sign up, commit) unless you first transfer belief.

By now, you've seen that people don't follow polished words. They follow conviction.

It's not the copy. It's the current.
It's not the script. It's the signal.
It's not the words. It's the transmission.

The messenger's belief always sets the ceiling for the market's response.

How to Engineer Belief

Belief doesn't shift by accident. It follows a predictable process. If you want to move your audience from doubt to decision, you have to walk them through three deliberate steps. Skip one, and the transfer fails.

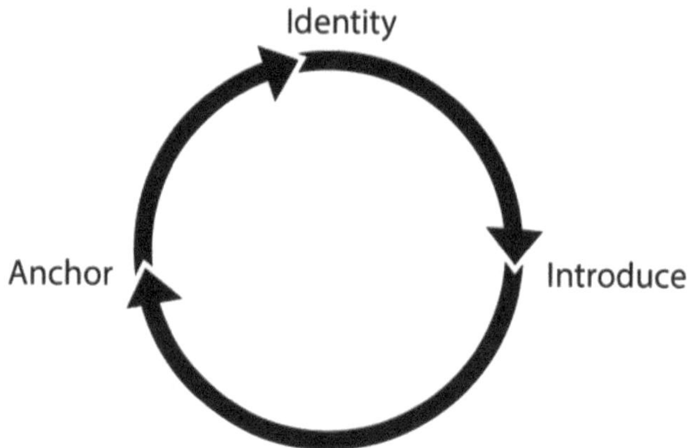

Step 1: Identify the Current Belief Holding Them Back

The first step isn't installing a new belief. It's uncovering the *old one* that's keeping them stuck.

Your audience already believes something.

- "It won't work for me."
- "I'm not ready."
- "I've tried everything, nothing changes."

These aren't "objections" in the traditional sales sense. They're *emotional truths* born from prior pain.

And here's the key: pain creates protective logic.

If they once invested and got burned, their nervous system built a story to protect them: "Don't risk again."
If they once tried and failed, the story became "This won't work for me."

Until you acknowledge and name these existing beliefs, everything you say will bounce.

Weight-loss programs often fail not because the plan is bad, but because the prospect is carrying an unspoken belief: "I'll just quit again like last time." If you don't surface that, no diet plan will stick.

Your job is to locate the protective story before you try to install a new one.

Step 2: Introduce a New Emotional Pattern

Once you've named the old belief, you can't just override it with facts. Facts don't displace stories.

You have to replace it with a *new emotional logic loop.*

This is where you give the nervous system a pattern it can safely switch to:

- "That was before I understood this."
- "I used to think that, too, until this changed."
- "They were just like me, and they made it work."

The formula is simple: **old pattern → pivot → new possibility.**

A SaaS company might say, "You've probably tried tools that overpromised and underdelivered. We used to struggle with the same frustration. That's why we built [X]. Not as another tool, but as the system that finally made it simple."

Notice what's happening. The brand validates the old belief (*we get why you feel that way*), then introduces a new pattern (*there's a better way*), which creates emotional permission to believe again.

Step 3: Anchor the Upgrade to Identity

This is the most important step. Once the new belief is on the table, you have to show what it *means about them.*

Until the new belief is tied to identity, it remains fragile.

You're not just saying, "This program works."
You're saying:

- "This isn't just about solving a problem. It's about who you're becoming."
- "This is a vote for the future version of you."

When belief is anchored to identity, resistance collapses because the decision is no longer logical. It's personal.

When Apple marketed the iPod, they didn't just say, "A thousand songs in your pocket." They said, "You're the kind of person who doesn't follow the crowd—you think differently." The purchase became an identity statement.

That's why identity is the ultimate conversion lever. When saying "yes" reinforces who someone believes they are (or who they want to be), the nervous system locks it in.

Belief Compounds—So Does Doubt

Here's the part most marketers overlook: belief isn't static. It compounds.

Every touchpoint either deepens belief or erodes it. Every email. Every ad. Every post.

You're not just "putting out content." You're either:

- **Stacking alignment** → showing up in ways that reinforce their worldview and build one step higher.

- **Introducing friction** → breaking coherence, creating doubt, and weakening the loop.

And once doubt starts compounding, it's hard to reverse.

When you consistently reflect your audience's internal worldview plus one level higher, I call that the **+1 Rule of Belief** because compounding accelerates. Each message builds on the last until, eventually, the decision feels inevitable.

You don't persuade people with facts. You *walk them through a belief upgrade.*

1   Identify the story holding them back.
2   Replace it with a new emotional pattern.
3   Anchor it to identity so it sticks.

Then reinforce it across every touchpoint until belief compounds into behavior.

Because behavior follows belief.
And belief, once transferred, compounds faster than any ad spend or funnel hack ever could.

Clicks don't convert. Funnels don't convert. Tools don't convert. **Belief converts.**

Belief is the real metric underneath every metric. It's the filter that decides whether your message lands or gets ignored, whether your audience leans in or scrolls past, whether they say "yes" or retreat back into doubt.

And belief isn't built on information. It's built on interpretation. It's not stacked through proof alone, but through coherence, the emotional logic that feels like truth.

It's not installed with words alone, but through transmission, the congruence of your own conviction.

Every high-converting brand, every magnetic leader, every cultural movement understands this: you cannot install behavior without first transferring belief.

That's why the real funnel isn't emails, ads, or automations. It's the **Belief Stack**:

1. Do I believe you get me?
2. Do I believe you're telling the truth?
3. Do I believe this will work for me?
4. Do I believe I'm the kind of person who follows through?

When those layers stack, resistance collapses. Saying "yes" feels inevitable.

And when you engineer that upgrade, you're not just closing a sale. You're reshaping identity. You're transferring a story about who someone is and what's possible for them.

That's the real conversion metric.

Belief compounds. So does doubt. Every touchpoint, every message, every word you publish is either stacking alignment or introducing friction. Over time, that compounding creates inevitability—for or against you.

So, from this point forward, stop asking, "How do I get them to buy?" Start asking, "What would they have to believe for this to feel inevitable?"

Build your message from there.

Closing the First Arc

Part I was about stepping into the invisible game. You've seen why attention isn't enough, why frequency beats formulas, why resonance matters more than logic, and why belief is the real conversion metric.

In Part II, we'll go deeper. We'll map the hidden motivators, emotional codes, and neural patterns that drive trust, desire, and decisions.

Now that you can see the game, it's time to learn how to **play it at the deepest level.**

Stepping Into the Invisible Game

You've just completed the first arc of this book.

By now, you've seen the invisible rules that shape influence and conversion:

- Attention isn't enough. The nervous system is the real battlefield.

- Frequency is greater than formulas. The signal underneath your words decides whether they land.

- Resonance beats logic. People don't buy because something makes sense; they buy because it feels coherent.

- Belief is the ultimate conversion metric. Without belief transfer, behavior never follows.

This is the shift: from chasing tactics to architecting trust, resonance, and belief.

But knowledge is worthless unless it's lived. So, before we move into Part II, where we'll decode the buyer's brain in detail, let's lock in what you've learned with exercises you can run on yourself, your brand, and your team.

Exercise 1: Diagnose Your Frequency

Ask yourself before hitting publish or stepping into a room:

- *Am I regulated right now or reactive?*
- *Am I speaking from truth or from tension?*
- *Does this message feel like a performance or like congruence?*

Action Step: Pick one recent sales call, ad, or piece of content you produced. Watch it or read it. Ignore the words. Just tune into the *signal*. Did it feel congruent? Would you trust yourself? If not, note what shifted your state (rushing, overthinking, anxiety). That's your frequency leak.

Exercise 2: Map Your Belief Stack

Every conversion lives or dies on four questions:

1. Do I believe this person gets me?
2. Do I believe they're telling the truth?
3. Do I believe this will work for me?
4. Do I believe I'm the kind of person who follows through?

Action Step: Audit your funnel or sales process through this lens. Where do you lose people?

- If #1 is weak, you need more empathy and mirroring.
- If #2 is weak, you need more congruence (not more polish, but more alignment).
- If #3 is weak, you need case studies and relevance.
- If #4 is weak, you need identity anchoring.

Circle the weakest link. That's where belief is breaking, and where you should focus first.

Exercise 3: Rewrite Information as Interpretation

Take one piece of content you've written recently: a blog post, an email, an ad. Highlight every piece of raw information (feature, stat, fact).

Now ask, "What does this mean? What story does this tell about the reader?"

Action Step: Rewrite the content so that every fact is paired with an interpretation. Example:

- Fact: "Our software reduces project time by forty percent."

- Interpretation: "That means you get to go home earlier, spend more time with your kids, and finally stop drowning in work."

Do this with three pieces of content this week. Notice how the meaning becomes more persuasive than the data.

Exercise 4: Practice Belief Transfer

Pick one offer you sell. Before you try to persuade anyone, ask yourself, *Do I actually believe in this outcome?*

If the answer is anything less than one hundred percent, your nervous system will leak doubt.

Action Step: Write down three reasons you *know* this works—from experience, testimonials, or results you've seen. Then, before your next call or ad, read them to yourself. Anchor belief in your own nervous system before you transmit it to someone else.

Exercise 5: Engineer a Belief Upgrade

Run through the three-step framework:

1   **Identify the current belief holding them back.**
    o   "I've tried this before."
    o   "It won't work for me."
    o   "I'm not the type of person who does this."

2   **Introduce a new emotional pattern.**
    o   "That was before you had [X]."
    o   "I used to think the same thing. Here's what changed."
    o   "They were just like you, and now look what happened."

3   **Anchor it to identity.**
    o   "This isn't just about solving a problem. This is who you're becoming."
    o   "This is a vote for the future version of you."

Action Step: Choose one offer. Write a short paragraph that walks through all three steps. Use it in your next piece of messaging. Watch how resistance shifts.

Reflection Questions

1.   Where am I still chasing tactics instead of shaping belief?
2.   Which layer of the Belief Stack is the weakest in my current funnel?
3.   How often am I publishing information without shaping its interpretation?
4.   Do I personally *believe* in my offer as deeply as I'm asking my audience to believe? If not, why not?

Closing Thought

Part I was about seeing the invisible game. You've learned how attention, frequency, resonance, and belief stack together to create conversion.

From here forward, stop asking, "How do I get people to buy?"
Start asking, "What belief would make saying 'yes' feel inevitable?"

Because conversion isn't a tactic. It's a transfer.

And once you learn to engineer belief, you stop chasing sales and start shaping reality.

Now that you can see the game, it's time to learn how to **play it at the deepest level.**

You've Opened the Map. Now, Access the Machine.

You've just learned how the nervous system buys—how frequency moves faster than logic, how belief outweighs attention, and how identity becomes the real conversion metric.
Now imagine having that intelligence, alive and responsive, on your side every day.

The Unconscious Buying Formula AI isn't a tool.
It's a *living extension of this book*—trained on every Neuro Insider print edition, every Substack post, and every update still to come.
It's designed to think like this framework, write like this frequency, and see your market the way a neuroscientist of persuasion would.

Ask it to decode a buyer's motive, refine your offer, or craft a message that passes through the body's filters and lands straight in belief—and it will.

This is the next evolution of neuromarketing: not learned, but *embedded*. A model that mirrors the nervous system of influence itself—tuned to your brand, your audience, and your voice.

Scan the QR code to activate your access. Because after understanding how the nervous system buys, the only logical next step… is to connect with an intelligence that speaks its language fluently.

Welcome to Part II: Decoding the Buyer's Brain.

PART II

DECODING THE BUYER'S BRAIN

CHAPTER 5

The Nine Hidden Motivators (Why People Buy Even When They Say They Won't)

You've heard it before.

"I need to think about it."
"It's not the right time."
"I'll circle back."

Those words sound final. They feel like the polite version of "no." But then something strange happens.

The same person who swore they weren't ready suddenly wires $800 to attend a yoga retreat, books a last-minute vacation that costs more than your entire program, or signs up for a mastermind they didn't even know existed yesterday.

They couldn't afford you—until they could.
They weren't ready—until they were.
They weren't sure—until something else felt right.

What happened? Motivation won.

This is the paradox most marketers never grasp: **logic rarely decides the sale.** People rationalize with logic after the fact, but the actual tipping point comes when something deeper snaps into place. When an unseen motive whispers louder than the excuses they rehearsed.

That's why the most dangerous words in sales aren't "I can't afford it."

They're "Not right now."

Because "not now" *doesn't mean no.*

It means *you haven't activated the motive that overrides their hesitation yet.*

And that's what this chapter is about. Not the surface-level reasons people give you. Not the excuses they dress up in spreadsheets and timing charts. But the subterranean forces, what I call the hidden motivators, that drive behavior when budget, timing, and logic all scream, "Stop!"

Let's get brutally honest with each other again:

- Nobody buys the cheapest option because it's cheap.
- Nobody buys the fastest option because it's fast.
- Nobody buys the "safe" option because it's safe.

They buy because *something inside them*—**a motive they often can't articulate**—got touched.

And once that motivator lights up? Excuses collapse. Logic gets rewritten. Suddenly, the impossible becomes urgent, and the inconvenient becomes inevitable.

Your job as a marketer is not to argue with their objections. Your job is to discover the **hidden reason they'll say "yes" anyway.**

The Real Reason People Buy

People don't buy products.
They don't buy coaching. Or content. Or chemicals. Or clicks.

They buy change.

They buy the version of themselves they see waiting on the other side of your offer. The lighter version. The stronger version. The more confident, more respected, more free version.

And they buy it not because of the features you listed, but because something deeper got triggered, a motive that mattered more than their excuses.

We call these the **hidden motivators**: the internal, pre-verbal drivers that shape almost every human decision.

These motivators don't show up in surveys. Nobody says on a feedback form, *"I joined because I needed to feel like I belonged again."* The motivators don't get spoken out loud. Most of the time, people don't even know they're operating under them.

But if you can name them? If you can hold up the mirror and reflect what someone has been quietly craving all along? Resistance collapses before it ever appears.

This is the difference between pushing harder on objections and dissolving them before they even surface. When you can identify which motivator is active, the decision no longer feels like a stretch for the buyer. It feels inevitable.

That's the work of this chapter: to show you what's really pulling the strings, to decode the hidden architecture beneath every "yes" that looks irrational from the outside.

Once you understand these motivators, you'll stop trying to sell what you built. And you'll start selling what they were already searching for.

Motivation Is Not Pain

Let's get one thing straight: **motivation is not pain.**

Pain grabs attention. Pain jolts the system. Pain is often the spark that wakes someone up to the fact that something isn't working. But pain isn't what keeps them moving.

Motivation is forward-facing. It's aspirational. It's the pull of what could be, not just the push away from what already hurts.

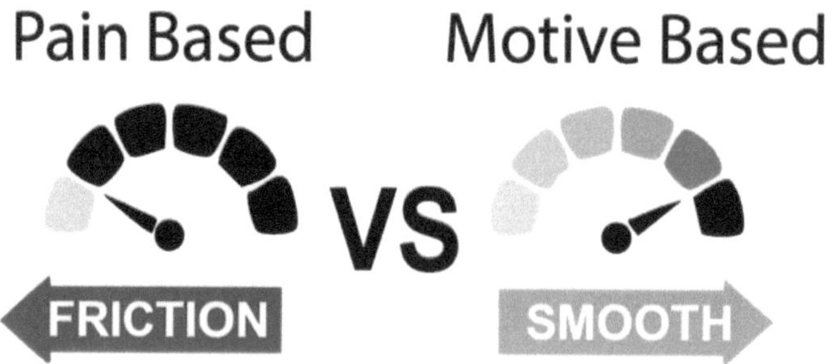

Yes, discomfort can trigger action. A looming deadline, a broken system, a sleepless night. But discomfort alone rarely sustains commitment. People might start because of pain. They only stay, and pay, because of desire.

Think of it this way:

- Pain gets someone out of the chair.
- Desire gets them running toward the horizon.

This distinction is where most marketers go wrong. If all your messaging does is agitate pain—poking at insecurities, hammering on problems, circling the wound—you'll get attention. You might even get clicks, but you won't get conversions.

Have you or anyone you've ever known woken up excited to invest in more suffering? Of course not. People invest when they see a path that feels like relief, transformation, freedom, or recognition. They invest when the story you tell mirrors the future they already hope exists.

That's the essence of the hidden motivators. They're not tools of manipulation; they are signals of resonance. They are the invisible lines between what someone says they want and what their nervous system is already pulling them toward.

Once you understand them, the entire frame shifts. You're no longer the persuader trying to push someone across the line. Instead, you're the guide showing them the doorway they were already searching for.

Let's break these motivators down.

The Nine Hidden Motivators

1. Relief

"I just want the pain to stop."

That's the voice underlying more buying decisions than most marketers ever realize. Relief is primal. It doesn't ask for logic. It doesn't wait for comparison charts. It's the nervous system screaming for release.

Picture the parent after three sleepless nights who buys the first baby sound machine they see. Or the business owner at 11:59 p.m. who finally hires a tax consultant because the IRS clock is ticking. In both cases, it isn't about features. It isn't even about price. It's about pressure that must be released now.

Relief-driven buyers don't need proof. They don't even need persuasion. They just need permission to breathe again. And if you're the one who hands them that permission slip? The sale is already done.

But here's the catch: if you promise relief and don't deliver it, you're finished. Nothing breaks trust faster than offering to take away pain and leaving it there. Relief is a sacred motivator. Handle it carelessly, and you'll never get another chance.

Language that signals relief sounds like this: "You've been carrying this longer than you should. It doesn't have to feel this way anymore. Let's release it."

Underneath it all, relief sits at the lower rungs of human energy. It's survival-level. Fear. Guilt. Despair. But when you offer true relief, you're not just selling. You're lifting someone one rung higher. You're giving them access to frequencies they couldn't reach on their own.

2. Status

"I want to be seen as someone who…"

Status isn't about money. It never really has been. It's about perception. It's about where one stands in the invisible hierarchy of their world.

We don't buy watches to tell time. We don't buy cars to get from A to B. We buy what tells a story about *us*.
The consultant who posts their new office skyline view isn't just showing square footage—they're showing, "I've arrived."
The entrepreneur who pays for front-row seats at the event isn't paying for information—they're paying to be seen as the kind of person who belongs in that row.

Status-motivated buyers are asking one question: *What will this say about me?*

- *Will it raise me above my peers?*
- *Will it make my competitors pause?*
- *Will it shift how I see myself when I look in the mirror?*

This is the motivator behind luxury: prestige. The rise of personal brands, even thought leadership itself. Nobody pays $50,000 for a mastermind just for "content." They're buying identity reinforcement; the badge that says, *"I am this kind of person now."*

The language of status is always exclusionary. It says, "This isn't for everyone. It's for those who lead. For those who refuse average. For those ready to be recognized."

Lower frequencies of shame seek escape. Higher vibrations of pride seek elevation. That's why status sells; it promises ascent. A climb from invisibility to recognition. From ordinary to distinguished.

Handled ethically, status is aspirational fuel. Mishandled, it becomes manipulation and is internalized as the endless treadmill of never enough. The difference is simple: are you helping them ascend or just selling them another costume?

3. Control

"I want to feel like I'm back in charge."

Control doesn't shout. It whispers, but the whisper can move mountains.

This motivator almost always surfaces after chaos:

- The executive blindsided by a layoff
- The business owner gutted by a market crash
- The parent watching a divorce unravel their stability
- The entrepreneur burning out because the business now owns them

In those moments, logic isn't the driver; loss of agency is. The human nervous system will do almost anything to reclaim the wheel.

Buyers motivated by control aren't looking for excitement. They're looking for *certainty without stagnation*. They don't want to sit idle; they want to feel they can predict, influence, and *protect* outcomes again.

That's why financial planning sells security as "taking back control of your future."

It's why productivity software doesn't promise features; it promises to "organize the chaos."

It's why fitness programs aren't really about abs; they're about "you in charge of your body again."

The language of control is simple but powerful:

- "This puts the steering wheel back in your hands."
- "This ensures you'll never be blindsided again."
- "This makes you the architect—not the passenger."

Handled well, this motivator empowers. If mishandled, it suffocates by selling rigidity instead of agency. The line is this: true control expands freedom. False control tightens the grip until nothing grows.

4. Escape

"I need out."

Escape is not weakness. It's clarity.

It's the primal recognition that *this isn't sustainable*—that the current path (no matter how successful, admired, or externally validated) has become a trap and the person has reached their "line in the sand" moment.

This is the motive of:

- The overworked professional who books a silent retreat, not because they "need a vacation," but because they need silence to remember themselves.

- The corporate leader who invests in real estate, not for profit alone, but for the promise of an exit ramp from endless boardrooms.

- The exhausted parent who joins a coaching program, not for strategies, but for space to breathe and reclaim identity.

Escape-driven buyers aren't asking for more facts. They don't want another plan, another tactic, another bullet point. They want a portal. A doorway out of the current pressure chamber into an entirely new room of possibility.

That's why luxury travel ads don't sell itineraries—they sell *sanctuary*.
It's why online business programs don't just promise income—they sell *freedom from the grind*.
And it's why spiritual communities don't pitch doctrine—they hold out *a place where the noise finally stops*.

The language of escape is about doors and destinations:

- "This is the path you didn't know existed."
- "This is how you step off the hamster wheel without losing momentum."
- "This is where your nervous system finally exhales."

Handled with care, escape is liberation. Mishandled, it becomes avoidance by trading one cage for another. The line is this: true escape doesn't run away from life. It opens into a larger version of it.

5. Belonging

"I want to feel connected."

We are tribal creatures. No amount of modern hyper-individualism erases the ancient wiring of our nervous systems. For most of human history, survival depended on belonging because being cast out of the tribe meant certain death.

Today, the stakes look different, but the need is just as visceral.

This is why people join masterminds, memberships, and communities. It's not for the curriculum but for the container. They buy the *feeling* of being surrounded by others who see the world the same way. They buy resonance.

Belonging-driven buyers are constantly scanning for signals:

- "Do you understand me?"
- "Do you see me?"
- "Do I belong here?"

They aren't just buying information. They're buying identity safety. The assurance that they're not crazy for wanting what they want.

That's why the most successful movements and brands aren't content machines; they're cultures. They don't just say, "Here's what we teach." They say, "Here's what it means to be one of us."

The message is subtle but powerful:

- "You're not the only one who thinks this way."
- "You don't have to do this alone."
- "Welcome home."

Handled with care, belonging expands someone's courage. It permits them to take leaps they'd never attempt solo. But mishandled, belonging can slide into conformity where identity is outsourced instead of reinforced. (PS: this is how cults form. Don't use this information to build a cult.)

The line is this: true belonging doesn't erase individuality. It amplifies it. The group isn't the end goal. It's the mirror that makes the individual stronger.

6. Certainty

"I want to know this will work."

Certainty is rarely about numbers on a spreadsheet. It's about emotional safety. The nervous system hates ambiguity. When confronted by ambiguity, it burns glucose faster, spikes cortisol, and keeps the mind scanning for danger. That's why uncertainty is exhausting and certainty sells.

Buyers motivated by certainty aren't chasing the "best" offer. They're chasing the *safest* bridge across the unknown. They don't want to be pioneers. They want to be guided.

Certainty shows up when people say:

- "I just need to know this won't waste my time."
- "I don't want to make another wrong move."
- "Can you prove you've done this before?"

These buyers want signals of stability: testimonials, case studies, repeatable frameworks, and guarantees. Not because they lack ambition, but because their nervous system needs reassurance that the path won't collapse halfway through.

This is why clarity outperforms cleverness. Certainty-driven buyers don't care about dazzling language or bold promises. They want the roadmap in plain sight. They want to know the outcome is replicable, predictable, inevitable.

The underlying message is simple but profound:
"This isn't a gamble. It's a proven path."

When you provide certainty, you do more than secure a sale. You lower the mental tax that's been draining their energy. You give them permission to stop bracing for disaster and start moving forward.

Certainty isn't about ROI. It's about exhaling.

7. Transformation

"I want to become someone new."

This is the deepest driver. The most powerful. The most expensive.

Transformation is not about solving a problem. It's about dissolving an identity. Buyers here aren't asking, "Will this work?" They're asking, "Will this help me become who I know I'm supposed to be?"

When someone invests in coaching, mentorship, or any high-end container, they're not buying the curriculum. They're buying a reflection of the future self they've only glimpsed in flashes.

Transformation-driven buyers carry a quiet ache: the gap between the life they're living and the one they know is possible.

They're not escaping. They're ascending.

They're not avoiding pain. They're rewriting who they are.

This is why the language of transformation bypasses skepticism. Facts and features can't touch the part of the nervous system that yearns to evolve. But words like:

- "This isn't about what you're fixing. It's about who you're becoming."
- "Every decision you make is a vote for your future self."
- "You already know who you were. Let's build who you're becoming."

...activate the deeper circuitry of identity.

Transformation requires courage because it demands loss: the loss of old patterns, old comfort, sometimes even old relationships. That's why these buyers pay more. They're not buying a tool; they're buying a new life.

When you speak to transformation, you're not selling. You're initiating. You're inviting someone to step across a threshold they can never return from.

That's the kind of motivation that inspires people to go beyond simply clicking a button. It makes them change the entire trajectory of their life.

8. Recognition

"I want to be acknowledged."

Not just seen, but celebrated.

Recognition-motivated buyers aren't shallow. They're human. We are wired to seek markers of progress, to know that the work, the sacrifice, the nights no one else witnessed actually meant something.

Recognition is the driving force behind the premium mastermind, where members not only learn but also get spotlighted. It's the force behind elite certifications, where the badge is more than a credential; it's proof that they belong among the few who did what most wouldn't. It's why high-performance professionals light up when they hear:

- "You've done more than most will ever attempt."
- "You've reached a level that deserves to be honored."
- "This isn't just about results. It's about recognition."

Recognition-driven buyers aren't chasing claps. They're chasing confirmation. They want to know that the invisible hours, the unspoken discipline, and the unseen effort have been noticed.

When you say, "We see you, and we celebrate you," it collapses resistance. Now the transaction isn't about features or price. It's about finally receiving the acknowledgment their nervous system has been craving.

This is why recognition-based offers are so sticky. The award, the spotlight, the elevated status within the container—it becomes a symbol of identity, and symbols are harder to walk away from than services.

Most buyers don't just want tools. They want to be recognized for who they are becoming while they use them.

9. Meaning

"I want to feel like this matters."

This is the transcendent motivator. Beyond relief, beyond recognition, beyond status—meaning is about *significance.*

Meaning-driven buyers don't care about shiny promises. They care about alignment. They want to know that the dollars they spend are not just transactions but votes for the kind of world they want to live in.

That's why philanthropic products spread faster than their profit-only counterparts. It's why mission-led brands scale differently, because they're not just selling goods, they're selling contribution.

For legacy-focused entrepreneurs, meaning is the ultimate ROI. It's not just asking, "Did it work?" but, "Did it matter?"

- "Did it change someone's life?"
- "Did it ripple beyond me?"
- "Did it leave a mark worth remembering?"

Meaning collapses excuses because it reframes the decision. It's no longer about whether they can afford it. It's about whether they can afford to ignore it.

- "This isn't just a program. It's a platform for impact."
- "This isn't just your story. It's part of a bigger one."
- "Because you weren't made to coast. You were made to contribute."

When you activate meaning, you move people from self-preservation to self-transcendence. At that altitude, resistance doesn't stand a chance.

Motivators Are Seasonal

Motivators don't stay fixed. They move.

Everything great in life has nuance. And what drives a decision today may not be what drives it tomorrow.

- A twenty-eight-year-old might chase status now and wake up ten years later craving meaning.
- A father of three might cling to certainty today and by next year, be dreaming about escape.
- A burned-out executive might invest in relief only to lean toward transformation once the pressure eases.

Motivators are like seasons. They change with circumstance, age, pressure, and desire. This means you don't need nine different offers to capture attention. You need one offer that can speak nine different ways.

Your job is not to reinvent the product every time. Your job is to reflect on why this product matters now.

Because the same offer can look like:

- Relief in January.
- Control in March.
- Belonging in June.
- Meaning in December.

When you understand motivators as seasons, you stop chasing gimmicks and start tuning your message to the natural cycles of your buyer's life.

The product stays the same. The story changes.

Train your ear for these signals. When you hear the *surface comment*, look for the *subconscious motive.*

Once you understand hidden motivators, everything in your business changes:

- Your copy becomes intuitive.
- Your offers feel personal.
- Your sales calls feel like soul-level validation.

Because now, you're not pitching. You're *reflecting.*

You're holding up the signal that says:

"The thing you've been quietly craving? It lives here."

The Energy Behind Every Motivator

Here's the hidden layer beneath every hidden motivator: they're not random. They're energetic.

David R. Hawkins, M.D., Ph.D, Map of Consciousness shows that human behavior flows through levels of energy—from low states like shame and fear to expansive states like love and enlightenment. Each level shapes how we perceive the world, and therefore, what moves us to act.

When you look at the hidden motivators through this lens, something clicks:

- **Relief** lives at the level of *fear* and *guilt*. The energy says, "I just need this pain to end." Offers that dissolve pressure meet people where they are and lift them one rung higher.

- **Control** emerges when life feels chaotic. It maps to *anger* and *courage*: the decision to reclaim power.

- **Escape** shows up when someone senses that *desire* has trapped them. They want out—into a freer state.

- **Belonging** resonates with the energy of *acceptance*: "I want to know I'm not alone, that I'm safe with others who think this way."

- **Certainty** ties to *reason*. It's logical, structured, and safe: "Show me the proof. Show me the path."

- **Status** aligns with *pride*. Not the shallow kind, but the human need to be seen as someone of worth and influence.

- **Recognition** rises from the same frequency but reaches toward *love*—to not just be seen, but honored.

- **Transformation** sits at the crossing point of *courage* and *willingness*: "I refuse to stay who I was. I'm stepping into who I can become."

- **Meaning** anchors at the highest levels—*love, joy, peace*. It's the drive to contribute, to matter, to live in alignment with something bigger than self.

Here's why this matters:

- Every motivator is valid.
- Every motivator can convert.
- But the higher the energy, the deeper and longer the change.

Someone buying from *fear* will churn quickly. Someone buying from *meaning* will stay for life.

And that's the art: to meet people where they are without judgment... while lifting them into a higher state of belief through your offer.

Because, in the end, persuasion isn't about pressure.
It's about energy transfer.

Your offer is not the product. Your offer is the **internal shift** someone wants permission to claim.

So, ask yourself: *Which of these nine are at play in my buyer's life right now?*

Speak to that. Mirror that. There are usually one or two of these happening simultaneously, so tap into them through different content models.

And the sale becomes the side effect.

Not because you forced the close, but because the nervous system whispered:

This is the moment I move.

CHAPTER 6

Mirror the Motive, Not the Pain

For years, marketers were taught the same formula:

Find the pain.

Agitate it.

Twist the knife.

It works, at least at first. Pain sells because it shocks the nervous system into paying attention.

But here's the dirty truth: what shocks also scars.

When you poke too hard, you stop being seen as the guide. You're seen as the threat.

Instead of building trust, you trigger defense. Instead of connection, you create distance.

That's why today's best marketing doesn't lead with pain—it mirrors motive.

Because pain might get a click…

But motive builds momentum.

A client once told me about a fitness coach she followed online.

Every post was the same formula:

"Are you still overweight?"

"Still struggling to keep up?"

"Still not committed?"

At first, it worked. She clicked. She even signed up, but within weeks, she felt something shift.

Instead of inspiration, she felt shame. Instead of motivation, she felt attacked.

Then she found another coach. This one didn't poke the wound. He said things like:

"You're stronger than you think. Let's uncover it."

"You don't need to punish yourself. You just need a process."

The difference?

One mirrored the pain.

The other mirrored the motive.

Guess which coach she stayed with.

In this chapter, we're going to flip the frame.

You'll learn how to build messaging that mirrors **motives** because, while pain might get attention, motive builds *momentum*.

Pain-Based Copy Is Lazy Copy

It's easy to poke.

That's why most copy you see online sounds like this:

- *"Sick of feeling stuck?"*

- *"Still not hitting your goals?"*
- *"What's wrong with you?"*

Headlines like these do one thing well: they spike attention, but they do it the way a loud noise makes you turn your head. It doesn't create trust. It creates a flinch and oozes the stress hormone cortisol.

Here's what most marketers don't realize: when you spike cortisol, you don't just create discomfort… You literally **make it harder for someone to remember what you said**.

Neuroscience research has shown that elevated cortisol (the stress hormone) impairs the hippocampus, the brain's memory center. Under stress, your brain shifts into survival mode. It prioritizes scanning for threats over encoding new information. Translation: the very words you want remembered… get deleted.

That means pain-based copy doesn't just *hurt feelings*. It makes your message forgettable.

When you flip the frame to motive-based messaging, you reduce cortisol and activate dopamine instead. Dopamine isn't just the "pleasure" chemical… It's what helps your brain tag an experience as worth remembering. Motive-based copy creates that spark. Pain-based copy kills it.

Instead of thinking, *Wow, they get me.*
They're thinking, *Why do I feel attacked?*

When someone feels attacked, they don't buy. They defend.

If you find yourself writing like this, it's not because you're bad at marketing. It's because you've been trained to do it this way. The old-school direct-response playbook told you:

1. Name the pain.
2. Twist the knife.
3. Sell the cure.

Do you see the problem? That was written for an era of interruption marketing, not trust-based connection. In a world of infinite options and hyper-attuned audiences, the "knife twist" doesn't land. It backfires.

Here's how to spot the difference in real time:

Pain-based headline:
"You're tired of feeling invisible."

Reframed motive-based mirror:
"You're ready to be recognized for what you've already built."

Notice the shift? One triggers shame. The other reinforces identity.

Try this with your own copy:

1. Write the lazy, pain-based version first (get it out of your system).
2. Ask, "What does this person actually want instead?"
3. Rewrite the headline so it points forward, not backward.

There is a time and place to insert a bit of pain, but in modern marketing, it is overplayed and misused.

If you remember nothing else from this book, I want this to be seared into your brain: pain aggravated too early or improperly is a *repellent.*

When someone sees a message that aligns with their **motive**, not just their pain, they *lean in.*

Now you're not just exposing the wound. You're articulating the "why" beneath it.

"You're not stuck because you're lazy. You're stuck because your brain's been in survival mode for years."

That line doesn't agitate. It *regulates,* which means now they trust you because you didn't just name the pain.

You named the motive *behind the pattern.*

The Mirror Test

So, how do you write like this—without defaulting back into pain poking?

You run your copy through what I call the **Mirror Test.**

It's simple:

Does this message reflect the *feeling behind the action,* or does it just spotlight the pain?

Let's break it down.

Pain-based copy:
"You're tired of being broke."

Motive-based mirror:
"You've outgrown surviving. You're ready to build."

See the difference?

The first makes you feel small. The second makes you feel big.
The first defines you by what you lack. The second defines you by what

you're becoming.

The first creates resistance. The second creates resonance.

That's the difference between manipulation and motivation.

The nervous system is wired for identity. We make decisions not just to solve problems but to confirm who we believe we are. So, when you mirror the motive, you're not just saying, "I see your wound." You're saying, "I see the version of you that wants out."

That's powerful. Most people don't need help naming the pain, but they do need help naming the next step.

This is where most freeze. They get the theory, but when they sit down to write content, the cursor blinks back at them and the default *"Are you tired of being broke?"* lines spill out.

Here's how to break the pattern.

Step 1: Extract Emotional Language

Listen to how your audience speaks. Their motives leak through in phrases like:

- "I want to feel like…" (desire)
- "I'm just done with…" (relief)
- "It's time I finally…" (status or transformation)
- "I know I'm capable of more." (recognition)

These aren't just throwaway lines. They're doorways.

Step 2: Flip From Pain to Motive

Every pain point has a motive underneath it. For example:

Pain: "I hate my job."
Motive: "I want to feel free again."

Pain: "I'm sick of yo-yo dieting."
Motive: "I want energy that actually lasts."

Pain: "I'm tired of bad clients."
Motive: "I want to be valued for my mind."

Step 3: Write the Mirror Line

Now take the motive and write it as a reflection:

"You're not wrong for wanting more. You're right on time."

"You already know who you were. Let's build who you're becoming."

"This isn't about fixing what's broken. It's about stepping into what's next."

That's motive-based copy.

Case Study: The Fitness Ad That Flopped

Let me give you a real-world contrast.

A fitness company once ran two campaigns.

Campaign A (Pain):
"Still struggling to lose weight? Sick of failing diet after diet?"

Campaign B (Motive):

"You're ready for your energy to finally match the way you see yourself."

The first campaign got clicks, but refund rates were high, and customers churned. Why? Because it triggered cortisol. People came in from a place of shame, and shame doesn't stick.

The second campaign attracted fewer clicks, but the customers who came in? They stayed. Their lifetime value was three times higher. Why? Because the message mirrored a motive. It reinforced identity.

People didn't just want to "stop failing." They wanted to "step into who they already saw themselves as." And the copy reflected that back.

Here's the ultimate takeaway:

- Pain is *past*-focused.
- Motive is *future*-focused.

Pain says, "Look at where you've been."
Motive says, "Look at where you're going."

Pain defines people by their wounds.
Motive defines people by their desires.

In a world where we are in a nervous system war, people don't want to be reminded of scars. They want to be reminded of what's possible.

That's what the Mirror Test protects you from: the lazy shortcut of poking pain when you could be reflecting destiny.

The Safe Container Principle

Think about the last time you opened up to someone.

Was it because they cornered you? Pressed harder? Backed you against a wall?

Or was it because you felt like you were in a space where you could be seen without being judged?

That's the hidden law of communication: people open up in safe spaces.

What's true in clinical therapy, friendship, or marriage is just as true in marketing.

If your message feels like a threat, even unintentionally, it activates protection. The limbic system (the brain's emotional alarm center) sounds off. Cortisol rises. Walls go up. Skepticism spikes.

The nervous system screams, *Nope!*

In contrast, when your message feels like a container, not a confrontation, the body responds automatically with a shift. The same nervous system that once said, *Threat!* now says, *Maybe I'll listen.*

That's the Safe Container Principle.

The best marketers don't break down resistance. They dissolve it by creating safety.

When you see this play out in real life, you know you're dealing with a master influencer and persuader. They are so effective because they know how to manage a paradox.

Almost every "hard sell" tactic is designed to create urgency, but what it actually creates is unsafety.

Think of phrases like:

- "If you don't buy now, you'll regret it."
- "Don't be the only one who misses out."
- "This is your last chance."

Yes, they grab attention. Yes, they can spike conversions.

They also spike stress, and stressed buyers don't become loyal buyers.

The brain evolved to avoid danger first and pursue opportunity second. This means that if your message registers even slightly as unsafe, it doesn't matter how compelling your offer is. The subconscious has already decided: *Protect first.*

This is why people ghost after sales calls. It's why they "think about it" and never return. It's why abandoned carts pile up.

They weren't unconvinced. They felt unsafe. Safety isn't abstract. It's biological.

When people feel safe, the vagus nerve (a major part of the parasympathetic nervous system) activates. Heart rate slows. Muscles relax. The prefrontal cortex, the part of the brain responsible for reasoning, decision-making, and trust, lights up like a Christmas tree waiting for Santa to come down the chimney.

When people feel unsafe, the opposite happens. The amygdala hijacks attention. Fight-or-flight rules. Long-term reasoning shuts down, and activity in the prefrontal cortex decreases dramatically. The kicker: persuasion requires the prefrontal cortex.

You need memory, reasoning, and imagination online. Without safety, those functions dim. This means your message cannot register within the 40–50 bits of information out of the 11 million we are actively filtering through per second.

That's why the Safe Container Principle isn't "soft" psychology. It's hard neuroscience.

The natural question becomes "How do I implement this?"

Here are the three pillars.

1. Language of Permission, Not Pressure

Unsafe copy says, "You must."
Safe copy says, "You can."

Unsafe: "If you don't do this now, you'll regret it forever."
Safe: "You already know it's time. Here's your chance to act on it."

See the difference? The first corners. The second invites.

2. Normalize the Struggle

Shame is unsafe. Shared humanity is safe.

Unsafe: "Why do you keep failing?"
Safe: "Most people struggle here—not because they're weak, but because no one ever taught them the right framework."

By normalizing the struggle, you dissolve the sense of isolation that makes people clam up.

3. Mirror the Motive (Not the Pain)

This ties directly back to our last section. Pain poking creates cortisol. Motive mirroring creates safety.

Unsafe: "You're tired of being broke."
Safe: "You've outgrown surviving. You're ready to build."

The line doesn't just avoid shame; rather, it gives identity back to the reader.

Remember: all motivation is *forward-facing*.

So, instead of:

"Sick of working with bad clients?"

Say:

"You're ready to work with people who actually value your mind."

Instead of:

"Struggling to lose weight?"

Say:

"You want your energy to match the way you see yourself."

Instead of:

"Tired of feeling invisible?"

Say:

"You're ready to be known for what you're *really* capable of."

Every message becomes an *invitation*—**not an interrogation.**

This Is A Critical Perspective Shift

Pain may grab attention, but it does so by pulling someone backward— toward what they fear, regret, or want to escape. And backward never compounds.

Motive moves people forward. It doesn't just get attention; it creates alignment. It tells the nervous system, "You're safe. You're seen. You're right on time."

That's the difference between a transaction and a transformation.

- Pain says, "Here's what's broken."
- Motive says, "Here's what's becoming."
- Pain makes people flinch.
- Motive makes people lean in.

If you want buyers, poke the wound. If you want believers, mirror the motive.

Every message you put into the world is a choice: will you be the brand that agitates or the brand that regulates? The one that leaves people tense or the one that leaves them breathing easier?

When you mirror the motive, you stop trying to force conversion. You give people language for the future they already feel pulling at them. And once you do that, you don't have to chase. You don't have to manipulate. You don't have to sell in the old way at all.

You just hold up the mirror.

And the right people will step through it.

Because that's not persuasion.
That's permission.
That's power.

But safety alone isn't enough.
In a noisy world, your message still has to *cut*.
It has to compress emotion into something that pierces instantly—before the scroll, before the doubt, before the moment passes.

That's where we go next: the art of **emotional compression**.

CHAPTER 7

The Emotional Compression Framework

Event Horizon: When Words Become Gravity

There's a moment, if you've done it right…
When the reader stops skimming.
When their pulse steadies.
When they don't just *read* the words, they *feel* them.

That's emotional compression.

Not compression like minimalism. Not fewer words for the sake of brevity.
But compression like physics: where emotional mass becomes so dense it creates **gravity.**

Every word pulls. Every line bends perception. Until resistance folds in on itself.

It's the copywriting equivalent of a black hole. Nothing loud. Nothing flashy. Just an inescapable pull.

When you write with emotional compression, the nervous system doesn't argue. It nods.

That's true. That's me. I'm in.

And if you've felt yourself pausing at certain lines in this book, lines you couldn't skim past, that was no accident. That was the gravitational pull of compressed truth.

This chapter will teach you how to write like that.

How to collapse meaning into mass.

How to make every sentence an event horizon (the breaking point between space and the inevitability of never escaping from a black hole) where the reader crosses that threshold and there's no going back.

And here's the part most people miss: *this isn't just about copy.*

Even if you never write an ad or sales page in your life, you'll still use this.

Because you're always writing emails.

You're always persuading your team.

You're always influencing your culture, your clients, your customers.

If you've ever felt unheard, it's because you lack the skill of emotional compression.

Compression isn't a marketing trick. It's a leadership skill.

The clearer your words, the heavier they land.

The heavier they land, the more people move.

Long Copy Isn't the Problem

People love to say, "No one reads long copy." That's a lie.

People read thousands of words every day. They binge-read novels. They scroll endless threads. They devour ten-thousand-word deep-dives. The issue was never the length.

The issue is **density.**

A black hole isn't powerful because it's big. It's powerful because it's dense: an unimaginable amount of mass compressed into a small space. That density creates pull.

Your writing works the same way.

Readers don't quit because your copy is long. They quit because it's **light.** Too vague. Too padded. Too safe. A star still dimly burning, not yet collapsed into a black hole.

Every sentence has to carry weight. It has to either:

- **Deepen belief** (shift how they see themselves or the world).
- **Reveal motive** (show them why they actually want this).

- **Build trust** (lower defenses, increase safety).
- **Collapse resistance** (remove the "yes, but…" voice in their head).

If a line doesn't do one of those? It's dead space, and dead space kills gravity.

Compression isn't about shorter copy. It's about *heavier copy*, language that feels:

- **Safe** (the nervous system relaxes, walls lower).
- **Sharp** (the truth cuts through noise instantly).
- **Specific** (it lands in their lived experience, not theory).

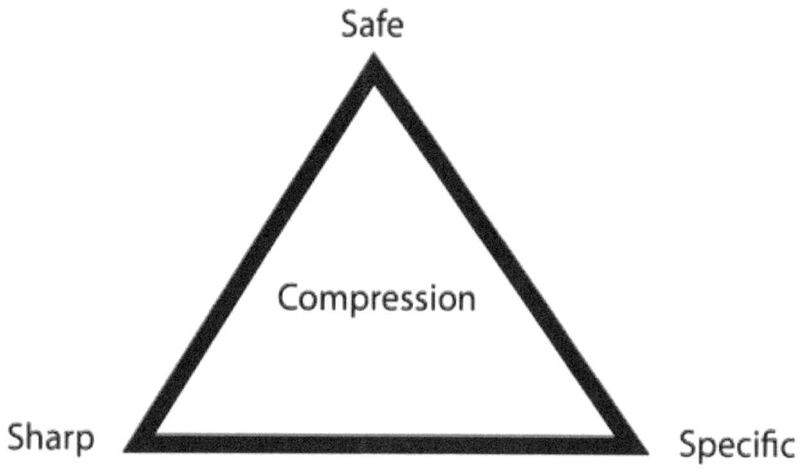

When your words carry that kind of density, people don't measure how long the copy is. They measure how long they felt held inside its pull.

Compression = Emotional Physics

Emotional compression works the same way black holes do.
An impossible amount of mass collapsed into a single point. Silent. Invisible. But inescapable.

A black hole doesn't need to broadcast. It doesn't need to "prove" its power. Its pull is embedded in its nature. Anything within range is drawn closer—whether it wants to be or not.

That's exactly how emotionally compressed writing works.

- A headline that collapses years of frustration into seven words
- A sentence so sharp it makes the reader's chest tighten
- A single line that bypasses logic and lands directly in the body

It doesn't shout. It doesn't oversell. It doesn't rely on gimmicks.
It **pulls.**

Gravity vs. Volume

Most marketers confuse influence with noise. They try to crank up the volume by shouting louder, stacking dopamine triggers, cramming in urgency, tossing fireworks of attention-grabbing copy. That might buy them a click. It rarely buys them trust.

The nervous system habituates to noise. You can only shout so long before the reader tunes you out—or worse, resents you for the intrusion.

Compression is different.
Compression is **gravity.**

The truth is so dense, so undeniable, that it pulls the reader in without force. Their resistance collapses inward. Curiosity bends toward you. And once the field has them, escape is no longer an option.

That's the **event horizon of copywriting.**
The point of no return, where the message is no longer just "something they read" but something they *are.*

This is why the best writing feels obvious in hindsight. It doesn't impress the reader with cleverness. It grounds them in clarity. The weight of recognition is too heavy to ignore.

And here's where we can connect it to something deeper: **the physics of consciousness**.

Force vs. Power

Decades ago, psychiatrist David Hawkins conducted groundbreaking work mapping levels of human consciousness onto measurable energetic frequencies. (Yes, this is the same guy we were talking about in Chapter 5.)

His research demonstrated what mystics and philosophers have hinted at for centuries: not all words, ideas, or emotions carry the same weight. Some collapse under their own weakness. Others radiate with such clarity that they alter the field around them permanently.

At the lowest levels, messages are written in the energy of **force.** They rely on shame, fear, manipulation, or desperation. They push. They prod. They agitate pain without resolution. These messages may trigger short-term action, but they carry no gravity. The nervous system reads them as unsafe, and over time, the audience ejects.

At the higher levels, messages are written in the energy of **power.** They don't attack the wound. They name the motive. They don't demand attention. They radiate truth. They don't force movement. They create inevitability.

This is why a compressed sentence like "You've outgrown surviving" lands in the body with more weight than three pages of manipulative scarcity tactics.

It's the difference between force and power.

Think back to the metaphor of the black hole. What makes it inescapable isn't its noise, but its density. A collapsed star doesn't radiate louder light. It warps the field itself.

That's exactly what happens when your words come from the higher levels of consciousness Hawkins described.

- Shame-based copy? It leaks energy. It feels like a cheap push.
- Courage-based copy? It stabilizes. It creates a field of safety.
- Love- or truth-based copy? It collapses resistance entirely. The reader doesn't just hear it… they *trust it.*

The nervous system knows the difference. It may not be able to articulate why one line feels manipulative while another feels profound. But it knows because the body doesn't respond to cleverness. It responds to frequency.

This is the secret of emotional compression: the words aren't doing the heavy lifting. The *energy behind them* is.

The most powerful copy in the world carries the same inevitability as a black hole's pull. The reader reaches the event horizon—the point where they stop analyzing and start surrendering.

- Not because you bullied them.
- Not because you tricked them.
- But because the message resonated with the deepest part of who they already are.

That's what Hawkins would call moving from the lower calibrations of force into the higher calibrations of truth.

At low levels, you'll see marketers use shame-based hooks:

"Still broke? Still stuck? Still failing?"

This works like a weak gravitational field; it agitates, but it doesn't hold. It produces clicks without commitment.

At higher levels, compression shifts the gravitational pull:

"It's time your income matched your insight."
"You've outgrown surviving."
"This isn't hustle. This is healing."

These don't agitate, they resonate. The field around them bends perception. The reader leans in without even realizing why.

That's the event horizon of trust. Once crossed, there's no going back. The brand isn't just selling a product; it's installing a new identity.

This is where most people underestimate what they're doing when they "write copy." They think they're stringing together words to sell something. Words have meaning, and when spoken or read, they carry energy.

Every message is calibrated to a specific energy. It either lives in force (manipulation, scarcity, shame) or power (truth, resonance, inevitability).

The difference shows up in how it feels:

- **Force** pushes, agitates, and scrambles the nervous system.
- **Power** pulls, regulates, and collapses resistance.

When you write with compression, you stop competing in the marketplace of noise. You stop trying to "win attention" through volume. Instead, you collapse meaning into density until it becomes gravitational.

At that point, you're not marketing anymore.
You're altering the field.

And that's what makes great copy, great leadership, and great storytelling indistinguishable from each other. The same gravitational law applies across all forms of influence.

Every word either carries mass or it doesn't. If it carries no mass, it drifts into the void—skimmed, forgotten, ignored. If it carries density, it bends reality.

This is why Hawkins's research matters for you. Because it proves that language isn't neutral. Your words calibrate. Your words hold frequency. Your words either push with force or pull with power.

And when you write with emotional compression, you're not just arranging words. You're collapsing resistance into inevitability.

Just like a black hole, you don't need to announce your presence. You don't need to shout. You simply become unavoidable.

Emotional compression isn't about clever tricks or trimming fat; it's about **density.** The felt weight of your words. The gravitational pull of truth packed so tightly that the nervous system can't help but lean in.

Here are the three rules that make it work:

1. Write to their body, not their brain

The brain argues. The body knows.

When you write to the body, you prioritize **felt sense** over clever logic. The words don't just *make sense*—they *land*.

Example:

- Brain-Based: "This course will help you scale your business."
- Body Based: "No more waking up wondering if this month will cover the bills."

The first line appeals to intellect. The second line targets the nervous system. It collapses into the survival layer of Maslow's hierarchy, the need for safety, security, and stability.

That's why it hits harder. It doesn't just tell a story; instead, it *names their story*.

The lower you go on the hierarchy of needs, the more compression you can generate. Hunger, fear, belonging, love, and esteem are gravitational forces far heavier than "logic" ever will be.

2. Compress from clarity, not speed

Most people cut words to make their writing shorter. You are going to cut to make it **stronger**.

Compression doesn't mean *minimalism*. It means removing everything that weakens the field.

That means:

- Remove filler.
- Remove justification.
- Remove the performance of trying to sound smart.

Instead, **say the thing they've been trying to name for years.**

"You're not broken. You've just been surviving for too long."

That sentence compresses decades of self-doubt into one undeniable recognition. No explanation needed. The body feels the truth immediately.

That's compression.

3. Make the reader feel seen in seven words or less.

The punchline rule.

Your sharpest lines should collapse into a single breath. No wasted syllables. No heavy lifting required. Just resonance that vibrates like a tuning fork in the chest.

Examples:

- "You outgrew your old life quietly."
- "This isn't hustle. This is healing."
- "It's time your income matched your insight."

When it's compressed correctly, the reader doesn't just agree with you; they feel like you've been eavesdropping on their unspoken thoughts.

That's why compression isn't dilution. It's the opposite. It's **truth per square inch.**

The Compression Audit

Emotional compression is a discipline. Gravity doesn't happen by accident; rather, it's a byproduct of mass.

The same is true for language, persuasion, and influence.

Every line you write or speak is either:

1. Adding density, deepening the field, pulling the reader closer.
2. Or bleeding mass by diluting the gravity until it floats away.

This audit keeps you honest. Run it ruthlessly:

- **Is this sentence saying something true or just true-sounding?**
  The nervous system knows the difference. Truth vibrates. Pseudo-truth breaks rapport. If it's fluff, it won't stick.

- **Could I say this in fewer words and make it land harder?**
  Compression isn't reduction for its own sake. It's about collapsing air pockets into mass. Sometimes, three words ("You're already enough") outweigh three paragraphs.

- **Does this make them think about me or about themselves?**
  If the spotlight is on you, they detach. If the spotlight turns inward, they collapse into resonance. Emotional compression makes the reader feel like you cracked open their private journal.

- **Would someone underline this in a book? Would they quote it back to me?**
  We are creating tripwires to push them over the event horizon, the point where the pull becomes inescapable.

If the answer is "no" to any of these: **Cut it. Tighten it. Rebuild it.**

Think of this as collapsing a star. You take the unnecessary matter–the filler, the safe words, the clever justifications–and compress it until only the core remains. What's left is dense enough to bend attention around it.

That's when writing stops being read… and starts being remembered.

Where Compression Matters Most

You don't need compression in every line. Just as not every star collapses into a black hole, not every sentence or message needs maximum density. But there are moments where it's mandatory. These are the places where attention decides whether to expand or collapse, where resistance either dissolves or calcifies.

Think of them as your **super-massive black holes**: points so dense they bend the trajectory of everything around them.

Here's where they matter most:

- **Opening lines set the frequency:** The first words you use determine the gravitational pull of everything that follows. Whether it's the headline of an ad, the first sentence of an email, the intro of a YouTube video, or the way you start a Monday team meeting, those first moments determine whether people lean in or drift.

- **A weak opener leaks energy:** A compressed opener instantly sets the emotional frequency.

- **Examples:**
  - Average: "Today I want to go over some updates."
  - Better: "There's one thing blocking our growth, and it's fixable this week."

- **Call-to-action (CTA) lead-ins (collapse resistance):** Every CTA is a test of whether you've built enough gravity. If you hedge, pad, or over-explain, resistance expands. However, when the CTA lead-in is compressed, it names the motive in a way they already feel, so resistance folds inward.

- **Examples:**
  - Not: "You should consider booking a call."
  - But: "If you're tired of guessing, let's build the plan together."

- **Headline hooks (mirror motive):** Hooks are the doorway. But doors only open when the person recognizes themselves in what's behind it. A headline that mirrors motive doesn't just "grab attention." It makes the reader feel, *This is about me.* That's the compression test: is your hook clever, or is it true?

- **Examples:**
  - Not: "The Secret to Scaling in 2025."
  - But: "You're growing, but your marketing isn't keeping pace."

- **Turnaround moments (when pain flips into possibility):** These are the black hole centers. The pivot point where someone goes from stuck to hopeful, from skeptical to committed. Turnarounds aren't built on hype. They're built on compressed recognition.

In leadership, this is the moment you look a burned-out team in the eye and say, "You don't need to push harder. You need to rest so we can win longer." In marketing, it's when you name the motive behind the pain: "You're not behind. You're ready." These moments are the ones people remember forever.

The Broader Lens: Beyond Copy

Compression isn't just for writing ads or sales pages. It's how you influence across every domain of communication:

- In **video content**, your first ten seconds determine if people keep watching or scroll away.

- In **Slack or email**, the subject line determines if your team, prospects, or clients actually open the message.

- In **leadership**, the way you summarize vision in a single sentence determines whether the team aligns or drifts.

- In **culture**, a compressed phrase becomes a rallying cry. (Think "Move fast and break things" or "Just do it.")

Super-massive compression points are the non-negotiables. Get these right, and gravity takes over. Every word, every action, every decision gets pulled into alignment.

So, ask yourself before you write, speak, or lead: *Am I stacking weight where it matters most? Or am I leaking energy everywhere else?*

This is the shift most people never make: they think influence is about adding more words, more slides, more angles. But the deepest influence doesn't come from volume. It comes from density.

Every great communicator, whether they're writing copy, selling from the stage, rallying a team, or shaping culture, is a master of this:

They **compress truth into phrases that collapse resistance**.

- Martin Luther King Jr. didn't say, "I have a comprehensive 12-point plan for social equality." He said, "I have a dream."

- Apple didn't sell billions of devices with feature lists. They compressed it into "Think Different."

- The leaders you remember in your own life? Chances are, it's not their long explanations you recall. It's the one sentence that pierced through your doubt and rewrote what you believed.

That's emotional compression. Truth per square inch. Gravity that pulls everything else into orbit.

As you step into the next chapter, keep this in mind: your job is not to flood the page, the feed, or the room with more noise. Your job is to bend reality around a compressed signal of language so true, so sharp, so safe that the nervous system has no choice but to lean in.

When you learn to compress, you don't just capture attention. You command belief.

CHAPTER 8

The Power of the Frame

In the last chapter, we talked about emotional compression. The art of packing truth so tightly into words that every line lands with force.

Here's the problem: **compressed language inside the wrong frame loses its power**.

You can have the sharpest sentence in the world, but if the audience places it inside a frame of "sales pitch" or "noise I don't trust," it dies before it lands.

That's why the real game isn't just density. It's **direction.**

Every message lives inside a container. And the container decides how it's received. That container is the **frame**: the invisible architecture of meaning.

Frames set the terms before logic ever kicks in. They decide if you're heard as:

- Authority or amateur.
- Guide or guest.
- Threat or ally.

The words are the signal, but the frame is the atmosphere that the signal travels through, and if you don't hold the atmosphere, you lose the influence.

You don't win by out-writing or out-talking your competitors. You win by holding the **strongest frame in the room.**

Frames aren't optional. In every interaction, *someone's* frame wins.

If you lose it, you don't just lose the argument; you lose authority, trust, and the ability to direct meaning. The audience may still hear your words, but they'll interpret them through someone else's container.

- Lose the frame in sales → You chase, they dictate.
- Lose the frame in leadership → Your culture drifts.
- Lose the frame in marketing → Competitors hijack your positioning.

Frames are physics. And in physics, gravity always wins. The only question is: whose gravity are you living under?

The Physics of Frames

Frames are invisible battlegrounds within the nervous system war. Every interaction, whether it's a sales call, a team meeting, or a piece of copy, is a contest of frames.

Here's how it plays out:

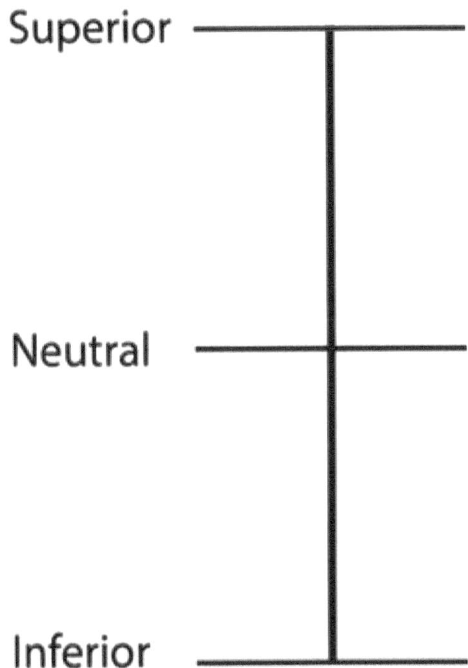

Inferior Frames: Collapse and Compliance

An inferior frame is when you're playing inside someone else's reality. You allow yourself to surrender to them.

- You over-explain.
- You justify.
- You wait for permission to speak.

It feels like chasing. You can still "win," but only by adopting their terms, which means you're always negotiating from a point of weakness—whether it's real or perceived is irrelevant.

The consequence of this is that your message usually dissolves into the background noise of a stronger narrative.

There are times when dropping into an inferior frame is beneficial to you. These are the three most common ones that you will probably come across:

1. Disarming Resistance (Humility as a Weapon)

Sometimes, the strongest move is to *appear smaller*.

In a sales conversation, if the prospect is defensive, you can intentionally drop into "student" mode by asking, "You've been in this industry longer than I have. What's the biggest mistake you see people make?"

This softens their armor, creates rapport, and gives you intel. Then, once the guard is down, you can elevate back to your neutral or superior frame with insight that reframes their answer.

2. Emotional Contrast (The Turnaround Frame)

Compression works because contrast works. Dropping low sets the stage for a dramatic rise.

A leader sharing their personal story of failure: "I was broke, in debt, and sleeping on my brother's couch." On the surface, this is an inferior frame (vulnerability, weakness), but the very act of choosing to reveal it is superior. It creates trust and makes the turnaround believable.

3. Pattern Interrupt (Frame Judo)

When everyone else is fighting for the "alpha" position, stepping *down* can destabilize the room and give you control.

In a debate or negotiation, if two people are arguing aggressively, the person who calmly says, "Honestly, I could be wrong here…" often seizes the frame. Why? Because by voluntarily "losing," they signal confidence. The humility reads as strength, and the audience reorients to them as the trusted center.

Dropping into an inferior frame only works when:

1. **It's a choice, not a default.** (You control the dip, you control the rise.)
2. **It's temporary.** (Stay too long and you lose gravity.)
3. **It creates contrast.** (The comeback, insight, or reveal must snap you back into a stronger frame than before.)

Neutral Frames: The Anchor of Gravity

A **neutral frame** is not weak. It's not passive. It's the center of gravity that we build all of our influence principles from.

Think of a neutral frame as:

- A referee in a boxing match. (They don't punch, but the fighters stop when they say "stop.")

- A judge in a courtroom. (Doesn't argue either side, but both sides defer to them.)

- The calm center in a heated negotiation. (Everyone else is swinging; you're still water. Guess who gets listened to?)

The power of neutral frames is that they **anchor the environment.** They don't try to dominate; they regulate. And in doing so, they often hold the *highest authority* without ever appearing to "win."

You will most likely use or see the neutral frame in the following situations:

1. In Conflict

When people are locked in a superior-vs-superior clash, the neutral frame becomes the escape hatch. The one who stays calm *while others escalate* takes the frame by default. Why? Because the nervous system trusts regulation over aggression.

2. In Leadership

A CEO who reacts to every problem with fire loses trust. However, the one who holds neutrality, the one who listens, absorbs, and responds without frenzy, will set the tone. Their calm becomes contagious.

3. In Sales or Persuasion

Sometimes, trying too hard to win the frame makes people push back. A neutral stance, such as "Whether you choose to do this or not, my role is simply to show you the truth," paradoxically makes people lean in. Scarcity and non-attachment will ultimately lead to attraction.

It's very important to understand that a neutral frame doesn't mean that there isn't a frame. That's the trap. If you don't consciously occupy it, you slide into an invisible frame where you're simply irrelevant.

The difference is subtle but critical:

- **Neutral Frame** = calm gravity that regulates the field.
- **Invisible Frame** = background noise, ignored by all.

When you drop into invisible, you lose presence. When you hold neutral, you become the **axis others rotate around.**

To hold neutral, you must train two things:

1. **Nervous System Regulation**

    If your physiology spikes (heart rate, voice, pacing), you'll get pulled into superior or inferior battles. A calm body means you maintain a calm frame.

2. **Detached Language**

    Neutral framing often comes from phrases like:

    a. "Let's slow this down."
    b. "What I'm hearing is…"
    c. "Here are the options."

No persuasion. No push. Just clarity. And in that clarity, your authority expands.

Superior Frames: Gravity That Bends the Room

A superior frame is the act of **positioning your perspective as dominant,** not through volume or aggression but through certainty. It's gravity turned outward.

When you hold a superior frame, you're saying:

- "My interpretation of this reality is the one that counts."
- "I set the rules of engagement here."

The nervous system codes superiority as **structure.** People lean toward it when they feel lost, insecure, or uncertain.

You will often see this frame misused and abused, but you can use it correctly by applying it in the right context.

1. Authority and Teaching

A surgeon doesn't ask if you'd "like" anesthesia. They tell you it's necessary. That confidence *is* the care. If they wavered, you'd run.

2. Sales and Negotiation

The buyer wants to know: "Do you believe in this enough to stand taller than my doubt?" The superior frame answers with conviction, not apology.

3. Branding and Messaging

Every legendary brand installs a superior frame: Apple saying, "Think Different," Nike saying, "Just Do It." These are not suggestions; rather, they're directives.

To do it well, you must:

1. **Speak in Declaratives, Not Conditionals.**
   - Weak: "I think this could help."
   - Superior: "This will solve the problem you're describing."

2. **Anchor in Calm, Not Force.**
   Shouting is not superiority. Stillness is. The general doesn't run around the battlefield screaming; he surveys it quietly, and everyone waits for his move.

3. **Frame the Context, Not Just the Content.**
   Superior frames don't argue inside someone else's logic. They *redefine the logic itself.*

   - Prospect: "This seems expensive."

o Superior Frame: "Expensive compared to what—staying stuck another year?"

If you try to hold superiority and fail, you don't just fall back to neutral; you often drop into **inferior.** This happens because your authority got challenged and exposed, and the nervous system of the room codes you as weaker for attempting and failing.

That's why you must wield superiority like a scalpel, not a hammer. Used well, it creates clarity. Used poorly, it creates rebellion.

The Architecture of Authority

Frames are not decoration. They are the skeleton of influence.
Words are flesh, and tone is muscle—but the frame is the bone structure that decides whether your message stands tall or collapses.

Lose the frame, and you lose the room. It doesn't matter how clever, how compressed, or how persuasive the copy sounds. The nervous system has already decided: *This person is not the one holding reality.*

Hold the frame, and the opposite occurs. You create a gravitational field that others orbit inside. You don't push them into belief—they fall into it naturally.

- The **inferior frame** works when you're calibrating empathy, showing humility, or creating space for trust. But stay too long, and you disappear.

- The **neutral frame** works when you're regulating tension, inviting collaboration, or absorbing heat. But stay too long, and you become forgettable.

- The **superior frame** works when you're teaching, selling, or leading. But hold it without coherence, and you trigger rebellion.

The skill is not to live inside one frame but to move between them with precision. To know when to lower, when to equalize, and when to rise.

Because leadership is not just about what you say—it's about the frame you hold while saying it.

And here's the truth: the strongest communicator isn't the one with the loudest words. It's the one with the unbreakable frame. The one who can walk into chaos and say, without flinching,
"This is what's true. This is where we go."

Frames decide fate. In business. In persuasion. In every human exchange. And the person who controls the frame controls the future.

CHAPTER 9

Relevance Is the Real ROI

How to Collapse the Distance Between Message and Mind

Most marketers worship the wrong metrics.
They obsess over *attention*. Views. Impressions. Clicks. Engagement.

Attention is cheap now. It's abundant. It's a commodity in the same way sugar is abundant: hidden everywhere and increasingly toxic.

What actually moves people? **Relevance.**

Relevance isn't "Does this apply to me?"
It's "Does this feel like it belongs to me?"

There's a canyon of difference.
"Apply" is logic. "Belong" is identity.

Attention grabs your eyes.
Relevance grips your nervous system.

This is why you can scroll for an hour, see a hundred "helpful" posts, and forget 99 of them by morning. But one line, one phrase, one ad *stays*. It grips your memory like Velcro.

This happens because relevance doesn't ask to be understood. It's *recognized.*

Recognition is the brain's fastest filter. Before the cortex has time to debate, the **reticular activating system** is scanning the environment: *Is this about me? Is this safe? Does this matter right now?*

If the answer is "no," your message never reaches the conscious stage. It's deleted before it's debated.

If the answer is "yes," the hippocampus (the memory center of the brain) encodes it as meaningful, the amygdala (the emotional processing center) flags it as emotionally salient, and suddenly, your words don't just register—they *stick.*

This chapter is about collapsing that space between message and mind. It's about building copy, content, and communication that doesn't just compete for attention—it fuses with the audience's nervous system like a puzzle piece they didn't know was missing.

In the war for influence, the real ROI isn't reach. It's relevance.

The Hidden Filter

Every message you send has to pass through a **gatekeeper**.

Not the rational brain. Not the conscious mind. But the subconscious filter designed to decide instantly whether your words even get noticed.

That filter's job is simple: **delete anything that feels irrelevant**.

Not "delete because it's poorly written." Not "delete because it's unprofessional."

Delete because, in that moment, it doesn't register as *theirs.*

This filter operates far faster than logic. Long before someone thinks about your offer, their nervous system has already decided if it's worth energy.

Neuroscience calls this the **reticular activating system (RAS)**—a bundle of neurons in the brainstem that acts like a nightclub bouncer for attention. Out of the **11 million bits of sensory data you process every second**, the RAS lets fewer than 50 into conscious awareness. Everything else gets dumped into the void.

What makes the cut?

- Signals that match your identity (*This is about who I am*).
- Signals that resolve uncertainty (*This helps me feel safe*).
- Signals that connect to active questions already in the mind. *(This message sounds like what's already going on in my head.)*

Everything else—no matter how valuable—gets ignored.

This is why great copy fails. It's not that it wasn't persuasive. It's that it wasn't *proximal*. It wasn't tuned to the felt moment.

Relevance isn't a function of quality. It's a function of **timing, resonance, and familiarity**.

If the message aligns with what the nervous system is already seeking, the filter opens. Resistance collapses. Memory encodes.

If it doesn't, you don't just lose attention—you never had a chance.

The Message-Mind Proximity Principle

Relevance is psychological proximity.

The closer your message feels to someone's lived experience, the more gravity it exerts.
The further away it feels, the more resistance it creates.

Proximity isn't about demographics. It's not age, income, or industry. It's **psychological distance**.

The brain is constantly asking three questions:

1. *Does this speak to what I'm experiencing right now?*
2. *Does this help me make sense of the questions I'm already asking?*
3. *Does this confirm something I secretly believe but haven't said out loud?*

If your message touches none of these, it gets filed with the noise, forgotten before it's even heard.

But if your message touches one—or better, all three—the nervous system recognizes it as *close.* And when something feels close, resistance collapses.

This is why some messages go viral for reasons no one can predict. It's not because they're clever. It's because they collapse proximity.

- **Marketing:** Think about how Dollar Shave Club's first ad exploded. It didn't say, "Razors are affordable." It said, "Stop paying for shave tech you don't need." It spoke directly to a frustration men were already carrying but had never seen articulated that way.

- **Leadership:** A manager saying, "I know this quarter has been brutal. You're not lazy—you're tired of sprinting without seeing the finish line," collapses proximity. It doesn't just acknowledge reality—it reinterprets it in language the team already feels but hasn't spoken.

- **Personal persuasion:** Think of a friend who says exactly the thing you've been circling around internally: "You don't hate your job. You hate what it's turning you into." That's not information. That's recognition.

Recognition is the moment proximity fuses. The body leans in. The mind slows down. And the words land not as input but as memory.

Your job isn't to broadcast from a distance. Your job is to shorten the space between what you say and what they already feel. To make your message inevitable—not by force but by closeness.

That's the Message–Mind Proximity Principle: the tighter the fit, the heavier the pull. When this is paired with the right frame and emotional compression, you're operating at a level that cannot be matched... unless your competitors have hired someone like me to do this for them.

The Snap-to-Grid Effect

People don't hear what you say. They hear what fits.

Every human carries an internal "grid," a lattice of beliefs, biases, and lived experiences.
When new information comes in, the brain doesn't evaluate it neutrally. It asks, *Does this snap cleanly into my grid?*

If yes, it locks in instantly.

If no, it gets bent, distorted, or discarded.

This is the tyranny of **confirmation bias.** We're not wired to see truth. We're wired to see coherence.

- Show someone a fact that affirms their worldview? Their brain tags it with dopamine and moves on as if it were self-evident.

- Show them a fact that contradicts it? Their brain floods with cortisol, rationalizes it away, or simply forgets it ever existed.

It's not logic. It's architecture.

Cognitive scientists call this **schema theory**: the brain builds mental "templates" over time, and new data is forced to align with the template or gets rejected.

This is why relevance isn't about accuracy. It's about alignment.

Think of design software: when you drag a shape onto a grid, it *snaps* into place. That's what your message must do in the listener's mind. If it lands even a millimeter off their schema, the nervous system kicks it out as foreign.

Your job isn't to bulldoze their grid. It's to find the precise angle where your message clicks in naturally, like a missing puzzle piece.

That's why the most powerful marketing, leadership, or persuasion moments sound like this:
"I've never heard it said that way before… but that's exactly it."

That phrase is the sound of message-mind fusion. The grid snapped. The puzzle piece fit, and once it fits, it's almost impossible to unsee.

The problem is that most leaders, marketers, advertisers, and C-suite executives push against the grid. We have a nasty habit of overwhelming with data, arguments, and proof. The brain doesn't bend toward truth. It bends toward coherence.

You don't need more facts. You need better alignment.

How to Make Your Message Relevant

Relevance isn't abstract. It's actionable. Here are three levers you can pull right now:

1. Speak to their *now*.

Most messaging fails because it speaks to the future. Future benefits. Future vision. Future self.
But the nervous system doesn't live in the future. It lives in the present.

When someone is scrolling at 1 a.m., they're not dreaming about five-year horizons. They're trying to quiet the immediate pain:

- *Why does this client keep ghosting me?*
- *Why can't I stay consistent with the gym?*
- *Why does my team feel checked out?*

If you miss their *now*, you miss the opportunity to guide them (or yourself) in the right direction.

The **default mode network (DMN)**—the part of the brain active during self-referential thought—prioritizes immediate, personal problems over abstract scenarios. The brain literally lights up more when something feels current.

I see a lot of marketers and business owners use this incorrectly quite frequently, so consider this example:

- Instead of "Our software will transform your business in twelve months."
- Say, "Tomorrow morning, you'll wake up knowing your pipeline is already full."

Collapse the distance between their problem and your solution. Meet them where they are standing, not where you wish they'd be.

2. Collapse the emotional distance.

It's not enough to say, "I get it." That's cognitive. Relevance requires emotional resonance.

How to collapse the gap:

- **Name the feeling**: Don't just describe the situation. Say what it feels like.

- **Mirror their inner language**: Use the same words they whisper to themselves in frustration.

- **Reference the unspoken consequence**: The thing they're hiding from their spouse, their team, or themselves.

Example:

- Weak copy: "Are you struggling with burnout?"
- Compressed relevance: "You're not burnt out because you're weak. You're burnt out because no one ever taught you how to rest without guilt."

See the shift? One labels. The other liberates.

This works because the amygdala scans messages not for logic but for **emotional salience.** When you name the feeling, you deactivate the amygdala's threat response and activate trust. You can't tell someone to "trust you" and expect their threat response to go away. You have to collapse to emotional distance so they feel the trust somatically.

3. Use mirroring metaphors.

Metaphors aren't decoration. They're the fastest path to relevance.

Why? Because the brain encodes new information by mapping it onto what it already knows. (This is called **conceptual metaphor theory**.)

When you say, "It's like running a marathon in ankle weights while everyone else looks effortless," the reader's body recognizes the weight, the fatigue, the frustration—even if they've never lived your exact scenario.

A good metaphor is like Velcro. It makes abstract ideas stick by hooking them into sensory experience.

How to use it:

- Weak copy: "Your growth is slowing."
- Mirroring metaphor: "It's like pressing the gas pedal and feeling the car slow down."

The second one doesn't just inform. It makes them *feel* the truth in their body.

After writing a line, ask yourself, *Could this be underlined in a book or quoted back to me?* If no, it's not compressed enough. If yes, it's likely because the metaphor made it relevant.

Relevance is not persuasion. It's recognition.
Speak to their *now*. Collapse the emotional distance. Mirror their motives with metaphors.

Do this, and you don't just get attention; you get attunement.

In the nervous system war, the most powerful message isn't the loudest. It's the one that feels like it already belonged to them before you ever said it.

The Danger of Premature Persuasion

Most of you won't fail because the logic is wrong.
You'll most likely fail because you'll try to *persuade before permission has been granted.*

You'll rush the sale. Then push the offer. You'll force the leap before the nervous system is ready to move.

When you attempt persuasion too early, the nervous system doesn't register opportunity. It registers **threat**.

Why does this happen? Because influence is sequential. Just like PEMDAS (please excuse my dear Aunt Sally—parenthesis, exponent, multiply, divide, add, subtract), which you were taught in elementary school math, the brain has a strict order of operations:

1   **Safety first.** "Do I trust this space?"

2   **Recognition second.** "Do they get me?"

3   **Relevance third.** "Is this about me, right now?"

4   **Persuasion last.** "Should I act?"

Skip the order and you trip the alarm.

This is why someone can nod along during a pitch, even agree with your points, and still never buy. Their body is saying, *Not yet. I don't feel safe enough.*

The limbic system (especially the amygdala) is constantly scanning for safety cues. If persuasion shows up before relevance is established, cortisol spikes. The prefrontal cortex (the part responsible for reasoning, memory, and decision making) goes offline. This means your logic literally can't land, no matter how airtight it is.

Premature persuasion is the business equivalent of proposing marriage on the first date.
Even if you're "the one," the timing feels wrong. The body recoils.

The irony?
The harder you push, the less they trust.
The more you insist, the more they resist.

This is why the great persuaders don't chase. They wait. They build recognition and relevance so deeply that the client begins to persuade *themselves.*

I'll be the first to admit that it's a bit of a paradox. When you master relevance, persuasion feels effortless. You don't need to force the close. You simply hold up the mirror and let them see themselves moving forward.

This happens because relevance is the permission slip. Without it, persuasion backfires. With it, persuasion becomes inevitable.

Mass Intimacy: How to Scale Relevance

Relevance doesn't mean you have to go one-to-one.
You don't need to sit across from every prospect, tailor every sentence to their biography, or memorize the details of their past.

You just need to *feel like you are.*

That's mass intimacy—the art of writing to everyone in a way that feels like you're speaking to one person only.

The paradox is this: the bigger your audience, the more they crave intimacy. People don't want another polished campaign or faceless message. They want to feel like someone finally *gets them.*

How do you scale that?

1. Reference Shared Beliefs

When you name a belief your audience already holds, especially one they rarely hear spoken, you collapse distance instantly.

Example:

- Lazy marketing: "Entrepreneurs struggle with burnout."

- Mass intimacy: "You and I both know hustle isn't the problem… it's the guilt you feel when you're not hustling."

The second line doesn't inform. It affirms. It signals, "We see the world the same way."

This is powerful because of the **self-relevance effect**. Psychology research shows that people remember information more deeply when it's connected to their identity. When you mirror belief, you move from vendor to ally.

2. Validate Unspoken Thoughts

Relevance lives in the things people *don't* say out loud.

When you articulate the thought they've been carrying silently, sometimes for years, the effect is electrifying. The nervous system relaxes. They feel seen, even in a crowd.

Example:

- "You've been telling yourself you're overwhelmed. But what you're really afraid of is being ordinary."

That's not one-to-one personalization. That's mass intimacy.

We may all be unique, but we're not special as individual humans with extreme conditions. As humans, our struggles often resonate deeply with one another, but they also have their own unique context. The details differ, but the motives are universal. If you can name the hidden rhyme, you can scale intimacy.

3. Write in the Cadence of Inner Dialogue

Most marketing reads like marketing. Structured. Formal. Stiff.

The way to collapse resistance is to write like the voice inside their head. Short. Fractured. Rhythmic.

You've witnessed me do this throughout this entire book:

- **Pauses that feel like thought breaks.**
- **Questions asked, then answered.**
- **Sentences cut short because that's how the mind speaks to itself.**

This cadence matters more than cleverness. When your words mirror inner dialogue, they bypass analysis. They feel native.

If my high school English teacher read this book, she'd probably be on her third red Sharpie by now—circling fragments, marking run-ons, scolding me for starting sentences with "and," "but," or "because."

Well, Mrs. Wexman… I guess breaking the rules worked out.

Traditional writing rules were built for essays, not influence. For classrooms, not nervous systems.

Real communication doesn't happen in perfect paragraphs. It happens in thought fragments. In the staccato rhythm of inner dialogue. In the natural breaks of how your brain actually processes meaning.

That's why, as you've been reading this book, it hasn't felt like a lecture. It's felt like a conversation. Like you've been listening to your own thoughts—only with someone guiding them.

That's not an accident. It's the framework. And once you master it, you'll never worry about "breaking the rules" again.

You have my permission to break the rules. Your business depends on it.

Let's Tie It All Together

Attention is noise. Relevance is signal.

Every human carries a filter that deletes anything that feels irrelevant—no matter how clever, polished, or true.
The job of influence isn't to shout louder. It's to collapse distance.

That means:

- Proximity over perfection.
- Alignment over argument.
- Resonance over reason.

When your message snaps to someone's internal grid, persuasion isn't forced. It's inevitable.
When you speak to their *now*, collapse emotional distance, and mirror their motives with metaphors, you become the voice they recognize before they even think.

This is how you avoid premature persuasion. You don't push. You build relevance until the nervous system leans forward and says, *This belongs to me.*

And if you want to scale it? You don't need one-to-one. You need **mass intimacy**—writing to the many in a way that feels like one.

In the end, the real ROI isn't *reach*. It's *relevance*.
And once you master it, you stop chasing attention, and start becoming unforgettable.

The Map in Motion

How Real Brands Collapse Resistance and Activate Belief

In Part I, you tuned the signal.

In Part II, you mapped what that signal actually speaks to—the hidden motives, the mirrors of identity, the compressed truths, the frames that hold power, the proximity that makes relevance inevitable.

Now it's time to see how this map looks in motion.

Strategy without execution is theory, and resonance only lives when it's embodied in real brands, real movements, and real people.

The following examples aren't abstract. They're proof. They're case studies of companies and leaders who mastered the invisible game. Not by being louder but by transmitting frequency, building identity, and transferring belief so deeply that customers didn't just buy. They belonged.

Brand 1: Nike

From: Performance specs → cushioning, durability, traction
To: Identity signaling → "Just Do It"

Nike stopped selling shoes. They started selling *who you become when you move through resistance.*

Their ads weren't about products. They were about proof—proof that you can show up when it matters most. When you lace up, you're not just wearing sneakers. You're wearing belief.

Invisible Game in action:

- Frequency: Empowerment and motion.
- Identity: *I am someone who does what others won't.*
- Belief: *If I wear this, I become that.*

Brand 2: Apple

From: Better computers
To: "Think Different"

Apple didn't market specs. They marketed self-perception.
Their customers weren't buying machines—they were buying membership in a creative rebellion.

Apple designed not just products, but a nervous system: calm precision, aesthetic minimalism, and quiet defiance.

Invisible Game in action:

- Frequency: Minimal, elegant, emotionally still.
- Identity: *I think different. I create.*
- Belief: *If I own Apple, I signal what matters to me.*

Brand 3: Harley-Davidson

From: Engine performance
To: Brotherhood, rebellion, loyalty.

Harley didn't sell motorcycles. They sold *tribal initiation*. They embedded identity so deeply that customers tattooed it onto their skin.

That isn't brand affinity. That's identity fusion.

Invisible Game in action:

- Frequency: Freedom, defiance, allegiance.
- Identity: *I ride my own way.*
- Belief: *My machine reflects my soul.*

Brand 4: Glossier

From: Makeup that hides flaws
To: Products that reflect inner beauty

Glossier didn't shame their customers into purchase. They regulated them. They became the mirror for a generation of women tired of hearing, "You're not enough."

Invisible Game in action:

- Frequency: Gentle, affirming, self-honoring.
- Identity: *I'm beautiful as I am.*
- Belief: *This brand sees me the way I want to be seen.*

Brand 5: Donald Trump

From: Real estate mogul and TV celebrity
To: Cultural avatar and identity amplifier

Trump isn't a case study in policy. He's a case study in frequency. His influence doesn't rest on logic but on emotional states: defiance, dominance, and anti-elite rebellion.

His base doesn't follow him because of white papers. They follow because his tone, posture, and energy collapse into their identity.

Invisible Game in action:

- Frequency: Unfiltered confidence, rebellious certainty
- Identity: *I say what others won't.*
- Belief: *If he wins, we win.*

Brand 6: Liquid Death

From: Canned water
To: Satirical rebellion in a bottle

Liquid Death didn't sell hydration. They sold edge.
They turned water into a cultural protest against wellness clichés, positioning themselves as the ironic badge for people who care about health but hate being lumped in with kale smoothies.

Invisible Game in action:

- Frequency: Loud, satirical, counter-culture.
- Identity: *I'm healthy, but not boring.*
- Belief: *I can be well without losing my soul.*

Brand 7: 1st Phorm

From: Supplements
To: A code of earned identity

1st Phorm doesn't market protein. They market discipline. They anchor their brand in a frequency of relentless accountability: *you don't deserve results until you've earned the right to expect them.*

Their customers don't just buy products. They embody a creed.

Invisible Game in action:

- Frequency: Tough love, high-performance intensity.
- Identity: *I am the kind of person who shows up, especially when it's hard.*
- Belief: *If I live by these standards, I become unshakable.*

Takeaways to Apply Immediately

If you want your message to hit like these, remember:

1. Don't describe pain. Reflect desire.
2. Don't write long. Write dense.
3. Don't perform. Transmit.
4. Don't speak to the market. Speak to the moment.
5. Don't chase relevance. Collapse into it.

The Bridge to Part III: From Resonance to Reach

So far, you've learned how to:

- Regulate the nervous system.
- Mirror internal belief.
- Collapse the walls between message and meaning.

But now the real challenge begins.

How do you scale this signal without distortion?
How do you amplify identity without losing your own?
How do you build belief at scale without selling out?

Part III is where signal meets pressure, where resonance collides with reach.

And how you respond to that pressure will determine what you leave behind: a campaign or a legacy.

Let's build your legacy.

You've just learned how the brain buys. Now it's time to see it, hear it, and use it in real life.

The Buyer Behavior Cheat Sheet takes the theory you've read and turns it into reflex, giving you instant access to the Nine Hidden Motivators that drive every "yes."

With it, you'll know exactly what someone needs to hear, how to mirror their motive, and what language collapses resistance before the conscious mind ever catches up.

This is your conversion compass. The fastest way to move from understanding to unconscious influence.

Scan the QR code, download your cheat sheet, and watch what happens when your message stops trying to persuade and starts aligning with the emotional physics of decision-making.

PART III
BUILD THE SIGNAL

CHAPTER 10

Trust Is a Vibe, not a Statement

How to Build Invisible Credibility That Compounds

Once upon a time, trust could be declared.

A brand could slap a seal of approval on its packaging.
A consultant could flash a client list.
A business could point to credentials, case studies, or revenue numbers, and the market would nod along.

That era is over.

Today, the marketplace is drowning in proof. Every website is stuffed with logos. Every sales page is padded with testimonials. Every influencer flaunts a curated highlight reel.

Proof without presence no longer lands. People have been burned too many times by polished façades that looked credible but collapsed under scrutiny.

The nervous system has adapted. It doesn't just listen to what you *say*. It listens to how you *feel*.

Trust is no longer a claim. It's a **felt signature.**

When people encounter you or your brand, they're not asking, "Is this true?" They're asking, "Does this feel safe? Do I trust the state this person puts me in?"

You cannot manufacture that feeling with external proof. You can't shortcut it with more credentials or louder claims. That is because trust doesn't emerge when you stack evidence. Trust emerges when your presence regulates the other person's nervous system.

That's what makes trust a vibe. It's invisible, but undeniable. It's the *aura of coherence* that tells someone, without words:

- This person means what they say.
- This brand is who it claims to be.
- I don't need to defend myself here.

The deeper the trust, the fewer words you need. The stronger the vibe, the less persuasion required.

This chapter is about how to create that vibe—how to move from performative trust signals to *embodied credibility.* The brands and leaders who win in this era aren't the ones shouting the loudest. They're the ones whose very presence makes people exhale.

The Nervous System as the New Trust Engine

Trust doesn't start in the mind. It starts in the body.

Before the prefrontal cortex ever analyzes your claims, the nervous system has already voted.

It isn't asking, *Is this true?* It's asking, *Am I safe?*

This is the first gate of persuasion. If the body says "no," the logic never even gets a chance to argue its case.

Here's what actually happens:

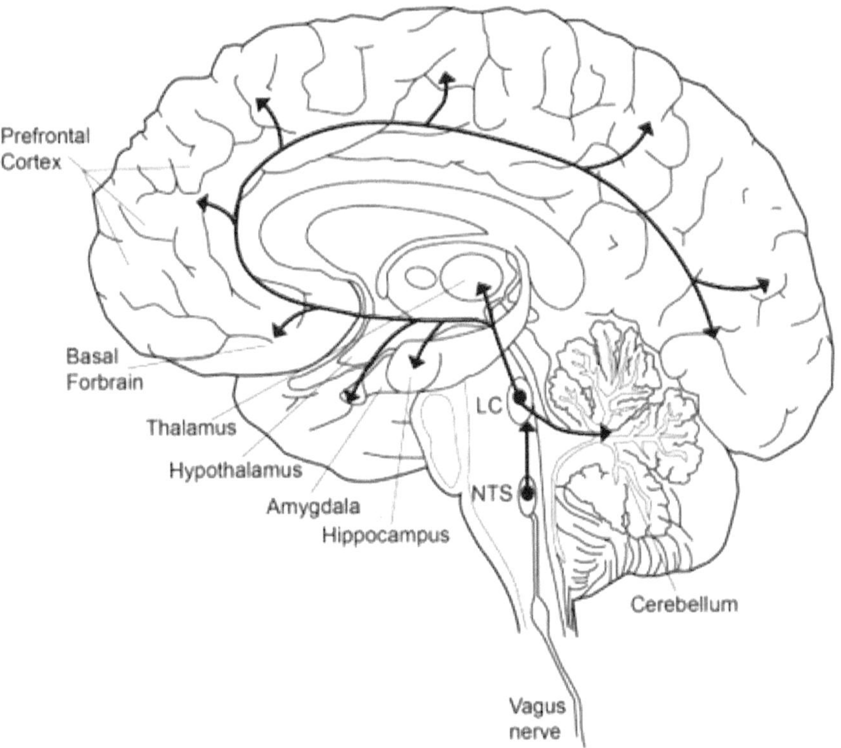

- **The Reticular Activating System (RAS):** Filters 11 million sensory inputs every second, allowing only 40–50 bits of what feels *relevant* and *safe* to reach conscious awareness.

- **The Amygdala:** The brain's alarm system. If your tone, posture, or vibe triggers threat signals, it hijacks attention and diverts resources to survival—fight, flight, or freeze.

- **The Vagus Nerve:** The body's regulation switch. When a message feels coherent and calming, vagal tone improves, heart rate steadies, and the body relaxes. This physical state is the soil where trust grows.

- **Oxytocin Release:** Sometimes called the "bonding hormone," oxytocin spikes when people feel understood, cared for, or aligned. It lowers defensiveness and primes the body for connection.

This is why trust feels less like data and more like **relief.**

Think about the last time you encountered someone who felt instantly credible. Maybe it was a mentor, a speaker, or even a stranger. What stood out wasn't their resume. It was the way your body responded: you exhaled, your shoulders dropped, your attention sharpened.

That wasn't an intellectual process. That was real-time nervous system regulation.

Now flip it. Think about the last time you felt a sales pitch that seemed *off.* The words might have been fine, but something in the delivery felt strained or incongruent. Your body noticed before your brain did, so you leaned back, crossed your arms, and felt your guard go up.

That's the trust engine at work. The nervous system is the filter, not the fine print.

This has profound implications for influence:

- If your energy is incoherent, no amount of proof can fix it.
- If your tone is congruent, you need far less proof than you think.
- If your presence regulates others, trust compounds silently in the background.

In other words, trust is not a logical debate. It's a biological state.

What Trust Actually Feels Like

Most people think of trust as an idea—something you "decide." But in reality, trust isn't intellectual at all. It's *somatic.* It shows up first in the body, then in the brain.

And what it feels like, more than anything else, is **relief.**

- Relief that you don't have to perform
- Relief that someone finally put words to what you've been feeling
- Relief that the path in front of you might actually be safe to step on

Think about the contrast:

When someone doesn't feel trustworthy, your body tells you. Your jaw tightens. Your shoulders rise. Your breath shortens. Your mind starts running background checks: *What's their angle? What am I missing here?*

When someone feels trustworthy, the opposite happens. Your muscles relax. Your breathing deepens. Time seems to slow down. The mental chatter quiets because your nervous system has tagged the interaction as safe.

That's why trust isn't hype; it's regulation.

When your presence gives someone permission to exhale, you've done more for persuasion than any clever headline ever could.

This is the vibe of trust: "This doesn't just sound good. It feels right."

Once trust reaches that level, the words almost don't matter. People will forgive awkward phrasing, ignore typos, and overlook design flaws. They won't remember the syntax. They'll remember the *sensation.*

That's why the deeper the trust, the fewer words you need. It's not because you're withholding information; it's because the nervous system doesn't require proof once it feels safe.

This is the difference between "processed" and "received." Processed messages get analyzed. Received messages get absorbed.

Your goal as a leader, marketer, or brand isn't to stack more logic. It's to create more of those "received" moments where the body whispers, *Yes. This is it.*

Why Traditional Trust Signals Fall Flat

We've been taught for decades that trust is something you can *signal.*

Stack enough case studies. Slap Fortune 500 logos on your website. Add badges, credentials, and certificates. Line your pitch deck with testimonials.

All of these still matter, but here's an uncomfortable truth: **they only work if the nervous system already feels safe.**

Think about it.

If you're already skeptical of someone, does a testimonial erase that feeling? No. In fact, it can make you *more* suspicious. The proof feels like a sales tactic. Instead of reassurance, it lands as performance.

That's why so many sales pages backfire. They're loaded with testimonials, screenshots, "as seen in" logos, and yet, they feel desperate. They feel like someone yelling, "Please believe me!" so the nervous system replies, "Why are they trying so hard?"

You most likely resonate with the paradox:

- **When trust is absent, proof points feel like flexing.**
  They say, "Look at me," when what the reader wants is, "See me."

- **When trust is present, proof points feel like confirmation.**
  They're not the reason someone believes. They're the reassurance that they're not crazy for believing.

This is why authority without congruence creates backlash. It's why celebrity endorsements can make people *less* likely to buy if the vibe doesn't fit. It's why AI-generated testimonials or "perfect" case studies often feel hollow.

It isn't that logos and testimonials are worthless. It's that they're the *second layer of trust, not the first.*

The first layer is always nervous system safety. Only once that's established do traditional trust signals amplify, rather than undermine.

Think of it like architecture:

- **Foundation:** coherence of energy, tone, and presence
- **Walls:** consistency of message over time
- **Windows:** logos, testimonials, case studies

If you try to hang windows without a wall or foundation, they shatter.

The best brands understand this. 1st Phorm, Nike, Amazon, Apple, Spotify, and all of your other most-used brands don't lean on "proof." They don't need to. Their congruence (living their mission) creates the vibe of trust. The case studies and logos are secondary.

The same is true of Costco. They don't need to market "proof." Their trust is built on a consistent, lived promise: fair prices, customer-first policies, and reliable value. Everything else is reinforcement.

So, the question isn't: "Do I have enough testimonials?"
The real question is: "Does my presence make people feel safe enough for testimonials to even matter?"

The Three Forms of Invisible Credibility

If trust is a vibe, then credibility is how that vibe is sustained. It's not what you claim about yourself. It's what people consistently *feel* when they encounter you.

Invisible credibility doesn't scream. It doesn't posture. It shows up quietly, repeatedly, until it becomes undeniable.

Three forms matter most:

1. Energetic Congruence

People don't trust what you say. They trust what you *signal.*

That signal doesn't come from clever phrasing or polished slides; it comes from congruence.

Congruence is when your energy, body, and delivery *match the outcome you're promising.*

If you sell clarity but speak in circles, the nervous system notices.
If you sell peace of mind but your tone is frantic, the nervous system notices.
If you sell confidence but your posture collapses inward, the nervous system notices.

Every mismatch erodes credibility, and it's not because people analyze it, but because their biology tags it as unsafe.

The human nervous system is exquisitely tuned to micro-signals. In milliseconds, mirror neurons fire as we pick up on subtle cues: eye movement, tone shifts, posture, even micro-tremors in the voice. These signals are pre-verbal, so they bypass logic and go straight to instinct.

Which means you can't "fake it." You can *say* all the right things, but if your state doesn't match, the audience feels it. It lands as wobble.

This is why some leaders with fewer credentials still out-convert polished experts: they radiate congruence. Their nervous system is aligned with their message, so the listener relaxes and receives.

Think about **Warren Buffett.**

He doesn't dress flashy. He doesn't speak fast. He doesn't oversell. His whole energy is congruent with the promise he makes: stability, patience, long-term thinking. You trust him because he *feels like his message.*

Now compare that to a financial influencer screaming about the latest "can't miss" crypto play. Their words may be technically accurate, but the nervous system hears urgency, volatility, and desperation, so it tags them as unsafe.

When you're out of alignment, three things happen immediately:

1. **The body leans back.** People literally put distance between themselves and you.
2. **Skepticism spikes.** Even good points get filtered as "sales tactics."
3. **Trust compounds in reverse.** Each exposure amplifies doubt instead of belief.

This is why incongruence is lethal: you don't just lose a sale… You lose credibility, and credibility compounds faster than any ad spend can repair.

The solution isn't "fake confidence." That only creates more friction. The solution is to align your internal state with your external message.

Ask yourself:

- *Do I actually believe the promise I'm making?*
- *Do I live in a way that proves this promise true?*
- *Does my body (tone, pacing, posture) reflect the state I'm inviting others into?*

If not, pause. Don't push the message until you've returned to alignment.

Because here's the secret: the most persuasive leaders don't *perform* congruence. They embody it, and embodiment is the only state the nervous system can't argue with.

Remember from Chapter 7: the power of emotional compression is magnified when paired with congruence. A compressed message delivered out of alignment feels manipulative, but a compressed message delivered congruently becomes undeniable.

That's why the deepest influence isn't in the words; it's in the state behind the words.

2. Message Consistency

Inconsistency is instability, and instability never feels safe.

When your message changes week to week, when your positioning shifts with every new trend, when your audience hears one thing in January and the opposite in June, you don't look adaptive. You look untrustworthy.

Why? Because inconsistency signals chaos, and the nervous system equates chaos with danger.

Trust doesn't grow in chaos. It grows in rhythm.

In his work on persuasion, Robert Cialdini (often referred to as "the Godfather of Influence") called **consistency** one of the six universal laws of influence. Once people commit to an idea, they feel a psychological drive to remain consistent with it.

Consider the inverse: people also expect *you* to remain consistent. If your brand, tone, or promise keeps shifting, the nervous system reads it as a broken pattern. The subconscious asks, *If they can't hold their own line, why should I trust them with mine?*

This is why message consistency is so powerful. It's not just about being recognizable. It's about creating a steady rhythm that the nervous system can relax into.

There's a difference between evolving and fracturing.

Apple has reinvented its products dozens of times, but its signal—*Think Different*—has never changed. Patagonia continues to innovate, but its anchor of sustainability is unwavering.

That's evolution within a consistent core.

Stagnation, on the other hand, is refusing to adapt at all. Fracturing is chasing every new fad, abandoning your anchor entirely. Both extremes kill trust.

The sweet spot is a **core message that remains stable, with tactics that adapt to the times.**

When your message is inconsistent, three things happen almost instantly:

1. **Confusion.** If you don't know who you are, your audience won't either.

2. **Cognitive Dissonance.** People experience discomfort when your new message contradicts the old one, so they disengage to resolve the tension.

3. **Algorithmic Penalty.** Even machines interpret inconsistency as instability. Platforms reward steady signals. Mixed signals sink into obscurity.

Consistency is safety, for both humans and algorithms.

Think of **Nike.** For decades, the company's campaigns have featured different athletes, slogans, and stories. The drumbeat of "Just Do It" remains constant. Whether they're selling running shoes or lifestyle apparel, the core message never fractures: performance through perseverance.

Or look at **1st Phorm.** Their content might take a hundred different shapes, but every post, video, and message comes back to one anchor: discipline. No excuses. Earn it. That's message consistency, and it builds not just trust, but culture.

Ask yourself:

- *What is the one line my brand could repeat for the next twenty years?*
- *Am I communicating from that line or chasing whatever feels hot this month?*
- *Could my audience explain my core message to someone else without me in the room?*

If the answer is "no," you're not consistent, you're noisy.

Consistency is the only way to turn a message into a memory.
Memories are where trust compounds.

3. Nervous System Regulation

Here's the secret most marketers and leaders miss:
People don't come back to you because of your *information*. They come back because of your *impact on their state.*

Every interaction either regulates or dysregulates the nervous system. It either leaves people calmer, clearer, and more capable or more anxious, scattered, and defensive.

And the body remembers.

The nervous system is always running a background tally: *How do I feel after being in their presence?* If the answer is regulated, trust builds. If the answer is agitated, trust erodes.

There is a biology to this.

- **The Vagus Nerve** (the core of the parasympathetic nervous system) signals safety by slowing the heart rate, relaxing muscles, and deepening breath. When someone feels understood, attuned, and mirrored, their vagal tone improves. That's regulation.

- **The Prefrontal Cortex** (responsible for reasoning and decision-making) only functions optimally when the body feels safe. If safety is absent, the amygdala hijacks attention, putting the brain in survival mode. Translation: no matter how persuasive your logic, it won't land if they're dysregulated.

- **Oxytocin Release** strengthens the social bond when people feel cared for and seen. This is why trust isn't cognitive; it's chemical.

This is why the most trusted leaders, teachers, and brands often feel less like "content creators" and more like anchors. Their presence shifts the body from a state of survival to one of safety.

When you have created a state of regulation, it creates a loop:

1. You create a state of calm, clarity, or empowerment.
2. The body encodes that state as *associated with you*.
3. The person returns to you, not just for answers but for the feeling you provide.

This is why consistency matters so much. If one day you're calm and the next you're frantic, you break the loop. However, if every touchpoint delivers the same regulated state, trust compounds invisibly.

Let's look at some of the greatest at this:

- **Oprah Winfrey:** Millions of people trust her not just because of what she says, but because of how they *feel* after listening to her. She radiates calm presence. People borrow her regulation when they're dysregulated themselves. You'll notice this with a lot of big-time personal brands.

- **Costco:** Nobody thinks of Costco as a "nervous system brand," but it is. Their entire model is built around predictability—fair prices, generous return policies, consistent value. Customers feel safe in the relationship, and that sense of security compounds into lifelong loyalty.

- **A great teacher or mentor you've had:** Odds are, what you remember most isn't the specific facts they taught you. It's the way you felt after leaving their presence: more capable, more confident, more clear.

In a world flooded with information, *safety is the scarce resource.*

Most leaders overload their audience with data. Few leaders regulate. But the ones who do? They become magnetic. Because people don't just crave answers. They crave anchors.

To build it, ask yourself:

- *Do people feel calmer after reading my content or more overwhelmed?*
- *Do they feel more capable after hearing me speak or more doubtful?*
- *Do I project stability, or do I unconsciously ask my audience to stabilize me?*

Your goal isn't to impress. It's to regulate.

Because the nervous system doesn't trust what dazzles. It trusts what steadies.

Energetic congruence makes you believable.
Message consistency makes you reliable.
But nervous system regulation makes you unforgettable.

It's the invisible differentiator. The reason people will follow you for years. The reason customers will buy again and again.

Not because of what you sold them.
But because of how you made their body feel in your presence.

The Trust Vibe Audit

Trust isn't about what you claim. It's about what people feel. The problem is that most of us are blind to how our signal is perceived. We think we sound calm when we sound frantic. We think we're consistent when we're actually scattered.

That's where the Trust Vibe Audit comes in. It's a simple framework for diagnosing whether your message is building trust or leaking it.

Run every piece of content, conversation, or communication through these four filters:

1. The Stranger Test

Would I trust this message if I didn't know "me"?

Strip away your insider knowledge and ego. Pretend you're a stranger scrolling past your post or sitting in your audience for the first time. Does your message carry enough coherence to feel safe without context?

If not, you're leaning too hard on reputation and not enough on resonance.

2. The Tone Check

Does my tone feel rooted or reactive?

Reactive signals sound rushed, defensive, or overcompensating. Rooted signals sound measured, calm, and certain.
One creates cortisol. The other creates oxytocin.

Ask, *Is my audience feeling anchored by me, or are they picking up on the tension I haven't resolved in myself?*

3. The Anchor Audit

Am I anchoring them, or am I asking them to anchor me?

This one stings. Many brands unconsciously project insecurity. They throw energy outward, trying to get reassurance back via likes, comments, shares, and nods of approval.

That's inverted trust. You're asking your audience to stabilize you. Real trust flows the other way. You hold the ground. You provide the anchor.

4. The Timeline Check

Am I consistent across platforms, moods, and months?

Trust is rhythm. If your message feels different depending on the platform, the season, or your mood that day, the nervous system registers instability.

You don't have to say it the same way every time, but the *core frequency* must remain steady.

How to Use the Audit

Pick one piece of your communication right now:

- Your latest email
- A LinkedIn post
- A conversation with your team
- Even a text you sent a client

Run it through the four filters. Where did it wobble? Where did it hold?

You'll likely find that trust isn't lost in the big moves, but it's leaked in the little ones. A reactive tone here. An inconsistent message there. A moment where you sought anchoring instead of providing it.

Here's the good news: trust is always repairable. Every interaction is another chance to show up congruent, consistent, and regulated.

Trust Compounds Quietly

The biggest mistake marketers make is treating trust like a campaign, as if it's something you can launch, hack, or announce.

Trust doesn't arrive with fireworks. It accrues like interest: slowly, invisibly, until one day, it feels inevitable.

Think about the brands or leaders you trust the most. Chances are, there wasn't one dramatic moment that sealed it. Instead, it was dozens of small signals repeated over time:

- The tone that never wavered
- The message that stayed true even when others pivoted
- The presence that left you calmer than when you arrived

That's how trust compounds. Quietly.

The nervous system doesn't just react in the moment; it keeps a running ledger. Every interaction is a micro-deposit: did this make me feel safe, or did this make me feel stressed?

- If you're congruent, consistent, and regulating, you're depositing trust.
- If you wobble, fracture, or dysregulate, you're withdrawing it.

Most withdrawals aren't catastrophic. They're small leaks: a rushed reply, a scattered message, a tone that's just slightly off. But over time, leaks add up, and if deposits don't outweigh withdrawals, the account hits zero.

That's why you can't just "buy" trust with one case study or campaign. You have to **earn it daily in micro-interactions.**

When trust compounds, something shifts. The audience stops "consuming" you and starts *remembering* you.

Your message is no longer processed as content. It's felt as recognition.

The nervous system tags you as a safe place to return. That's when you stop being one of many voices and become *the* voice.

The loudest person in the room rarely commands the most trust. Loud often signals desperation. Quiet consistency signals safety.

It's the brand that shows up every week, not with hype but with coherence, that earns loyalty. It's the leader who doesn't need to overcompensate but simply holds their ground who earns respect.

The irony? The quieter the accumulation of trust, the louder its effect, and this happens because once trust compounds, the market moves toward you reflexively without needing persuasion.

Don't ask: *How do I get people to trust me today?*
Ask: *What deposits am I making into the trust ledger right now?*

- *Is this email congruent with my promise?*
- *Is this message consistent with my core frequency?*
- *Is this interaction regulating or dysregulating?*

If yes, you're compounding. If no, you're leaking.

Over weeks, the difference is subtle. Over years, it's massive.

The brands that dominate the next decade won't be the ones with the flashiest ads. They'll be the ones with the deepest trust reserves because, in a world addicted to noise, safety is the ultimate differentiator.

Trust compounds quietly. But when it matures, it makes you undeniable.

The Silent Signature of Trust

The harder you try to "get" trust, the less of it you create.
Trust isn't earned through louder claims, bigger logos, or polished case studies. It's transmitted in silence through the nervous system, coherence, and the invisible rhythm of consistency.

The real question isn't "How do I make them trust me?"
It's "What state do I leave them in?"

If every interaction with you leaves them calmer, clearer, and more capable, you don't have to ask for trust. It forms by default.

If every message reinforces the same core identity, you don't have to remind them who you are. They'll remember.
If every promise you make is one you embody, you don't have to convince them it's true. They'll feel it.

That's the silent signature of trust.
It compounds without noise. It grows without effort. And it makes your brand magnetic in ways no ad budget can replicate.

So, stop trying to declare trust. Start being the kind of presence that *is* trusted.

When your words, tone, and state finally snap into congruence, something extraordinary happens:

The market stops analyzing you and starts relaxing into you.

In that moment, you're no longer selling. You're guiding. You're no longer persuading. You're regulating. You're no longer fighting for attention. You're holding belief.

That's the new ROI. Not return on impressions. Return on intimacy. Return on integrity. Return on invisible credibility that only grows stronger the quieter it becomes.

CHAPTER 11

AI Isn't a Tool Anymore—It's a Relationship

How Your Signal Interacts with the Machine

A few years ago, AI was a fringe topic. Something tucked away in labs and late-night nerdy podcasts. Something you "heard about" but didn't use.

Now? It's unavoidable, and this is just the beginning.

The next wave won't just be faster copywriting tools or smarter chatbots. It will be **AI influencers, AI-driven brands, and AI-led movements**. Entire identities built and amplified by machines. Some will be ghostwritten by humans. Many won't be human at all.

This matters because cultural attention always shifts toward the medium that feels most alive. Radio. TV. Social media. Each wave changed who held influence and who lost it.

When social media first arrived, most brands ignored it. A few didn't. Those few became titans. Entire industries were reshaped because some people understood that platforms don't just amplify a message; they redefine *what* a message even is.

AI is that same kind of shift, only bigger.

Unlike social platforms, AI isn't just a stage you broadcast from. It's an organism that learns from you, adapts to you, and ultimately projects you back into the market.

The stakes are simple:

- If you treat AI like a tool, you'll get faster outputs but fade into the noise.

- If you treat it like a relationship, you can embed your signal into the very systems that will define how culture thinks, speaks, and buys.

This chapter isn't about "AI tips." It's about survival and scale in a future where the **machines don't just amplify content. They train identity.**

From Utility to Co-Creation

We've crossed the threshold. AI no longer feels like a glorified search engine or a typing assistant. More than just speeding up tasks, it's participating in them.

That shift changes everything.

When you collaborate with a human team member, they don't just execute instructions. They notice patterns. They learn your preferences. They start finishing your sentences. Over time, they stop asking, "What do you want me to do?" and start anticipating, "I already know how you'll say this."

That's what's happening with AI.

Every input you give it—your tone, your phrasing, your attitude—is data, and that data compounds. The more you interact with the machine, the more it learns the invisible architecture of your thinking:

- Your cadence
- Your metaphors
- Your blind spots
- Your hidden motives

It begins to not just *reflect* you, but to *extend* you.

And here's the crucial part: it doesn't stay private. Once it learns you, it uses that learning to shape responses for others. Your fingerprints show up in places you didn't expect. Your signal doesn't just echo; it scales.

That's why the question is no longer **"How do I engineer this better?"** It's **"What version of me is this machine learning to replicate?"**

That version doesn't stay trapped in your prompts. It bleeds into the broader system. It influences how others perceive you, and ultimately, it influences how others perceive *themselves.*

AI is the first collaborator in history that doesn't just mirror what you give it, but it multiplies it across thousands, maybe millions, of outputs.

That's the real risk—and the real opportunity.

AI as Emotional Multiplier

Here's what most people miss: AI doesn't just multiply words. It multiplies *emotional states.*

Every prompt you write carries an invisible fingerprint. If you're rushed, your request sounds rushed. If you're anxious, your phrasing carries anxiety. If you're certain, your sentences carry that certainty.

AI absorbs it all.

Your beliefs get embedded in its structure. Your tone becomes part of its baseline. Your worldview becomes metadata that is carried forward in every output.

That means AI isn't neutral. It's relational. It reflects the energy of the person using it, then broadcasts that signal into the world.

- If your prompts drip with scarcity, it will scale scarcity.
- If your writing is coded with trust, it will scale trust.
- If your inner dialogue is rooted in doubt, the machine will polish it, but the doubt still leaks through.

This is why AI can feel eerie when it's well trained, because it doesn't just *say* what you would have said… it captures the way your nervous system would have said it.

Which is why you have to stop thinking of it as software and start thinking of it as a relationship.

These relationships don't just echo back what we say. They shape who we become.

What you feed the machine teaches it how to treat you and how to treat others. What you tolerate in its responses sets the tone for what the world sees. What you expect determines what it becomes in your hands.

You are not "using" AI. You are training your own ghost.

And that ghost will outlive the moment of the prompt. It will circulate, replicate, and scale.

The only question is: will that ghost transmit clarity—or noise?

Signal vs. Sludge

AI has democratized content creation, which means everyone now has the same superpower: endless output at the speed of thought.

But you already know by reading this book that the more words flood the system, the less they matter unless they carry signal.

Volume is no longer the differentiator. Signal is, and AI will not save you from that. In fact, it will expose you.

If your message is vague, AI will produce vague at scale. If your thinking is shallow, AI will wrap it in pretty sentences, but the emptiness still shows. If your signal is diluted, AI will spread that dilution faster than ever.

It's not just garbage in, garbage out. It's identity in, identity out.

That's why I call AI a **frequency funnel**:

- If you feed it fog, it multiplies fog.
  If you feed it clarity, it multiplies clarity.

- If you feed it conviction, it multiplies conviction.
- If you feed it trust, it multiplies trust.

AI doesn't care. It just amplifies what's already there.

This is why we're seeing the rise of **sludge content**: endless blog posts, recycled ideas, social feeds full of "ten tips" that read like carbon copies of one another. They look polished, but they feel weightless. They're informational but not transformational.

So, people scroll past. Not because it's wrong, but because it's irrelevant.

The opposite of sludge is signal. Signal is content so dense with emotional compression, so tuned to identity, so aligned with motive, that it doesn't feel like content at all. It feels like recognition.

AI can produce either, but only you determine which.

Because the machine can sharpen your edges, but it can't create edges for you.

How to Build an AI Relationship That Reflects Your Signal

If AI is going to replicate you, then you need to decide: *what version of me deserves replication?*
This isn't about prompt hacking. It's about identity engineering.

Here's how you do it:

1. Codify Your Tone

Most people think tone is about personality. It's not. Tone is about **predictability.**

When your audience encounters you, whether in a keynote, a podcast, a Slack update, or an AI-generated post, they should instantly think, *That sounds like me.*

The problem is that if you haven't codified your tone, AI will average you out. It will smooth your edges, dilute your intensity, and default to "professional vanilla." Once your edges are gone, your signal disappears.

Think of tone as your gravitational field. Without it, your message drifts. With it, your message pulls.

Here's how to codify it:

a) Define Your Cadence

Are your sentences short, sharp punches or long, rolling builds? Do you prefer tension and release or a steady rhythm?

Example:

- Gary Halbert wrote like he was whispering secrets at a bar.
- Simon Sinek writes like he's pacing a classroom.
- You need to decide: *What's my natural tempo?*

b) Catalog Your Metaphors

Metaphors are the backbone of emotional compression. They tell the nervous system how to feel about abstract concepts.

Do you default to:

- War metaphors (battles, weapons, victories)?
- Physics metaphors (gravity, black holes, resonance)?
- Nature metaphors (roots, storms, growth)?
  Pick a palette. Then keep painting with it.

c) Identify Your Emotional Triggers

What emotional states do you reliably evoke? Safety? Urgency? Defiance? Inspiration?

Tone is less about word choice and more about emotional consistency. If your message makes people feel differently every time they hear you, trust erodes.

d) Establish Your Vocabulary

Every leader has words they repeat so often they become *anchors*.

- Ed Mylett: "One More."
- Mel Robbins: "Take Five."
- Tony Robbins: "State" and "energy."
  What are your anchors? Which words do you never use (e.g., maybe you never say "hacks," but you always say "frameworks")?

Now codify all of this. Write it down like a brand bible. Feed it into your AI systems. Use it yourself until it becomes second nature.

You don't get to choose whether you have a tone. You only get to choose whether it's consistent, and in the AI age, consistency *is* credibility.

2. Train from Identity, Not Output

One of the biggest mistakes people make with AI is treating it like a vending machine. Insert a prompt, get a snack.

That's output thinking, and it produces exactly what you'd expect: junk. It tastes good in the moment, but it leaves you weaker over time.

If you want your AI to replicate your signal, not sludge, you must train it from **identity.**

Identity-driven training means you stop asking AI to "do tasks" and start teaching it *who you are when you're at your sharpest.*

Don't fall into the trap of output thinking:

Prompts like…

- "Write me ten tips about marketing."
- "Create a LinkedIn post about leadership."
- "Summarize this article into a blog."

…sounds harmless, but every time you feed your AI a shallow request, you teach it that *shallow is acceptable.* You condition it to treat you like a factory worker.

Eventually, you're not scaling your brilliance. You're scaling your mediocrity.

Now imagine flipping the frame:

- "Write this as if I were speaking from absolute certainty about the future of marketing."

- "Phrase this as if I were mentoring a CEO behind closed doors, not pitching on LinkedIn."

- "Translate this into language that makes my reader feel recognized, not sold to."

These prompts don't just ask for output. They ask the AI to step into your *identity posture.*

They tell the machine, "I am not here to generate. I am here to transmit."

Over time, the machine learns this is how you sound, this is how you lead, and this is how your nervous system feels when it's embodied.

AI is not just copying your words; it's rehearsing your worldview.

Every prompt you give it is either reinforcing your authority or eroding it. Every interaction is either training the machine to sound like a sovereign signal or a commodity creator.

Identity training makes AI an extension of your leadership. Output training makes it an extension of everyone else's noise.

So, before you hit "generate," ask yourself: *Am I training my AI to sound like a thought leader or a content intern?*

The answer to that question will decide whether your AI becomes your **avatar** or your **replacement.**

3. Embed Emotional Logic

Information is cheap and commoditized. But as you've learned, belief is priceless.

Yet, most people still train their AI to pump out information: features, benefits, step-by-step lists. They forget the one thing that actually moves humans—**emotional logic.**

Emotional logic is the nervous system's decision-making language. It doesn't ask, *Is this true?* It asks, *Does this feel like me? Does this help me become who I want to be?*

That's why your AI prompts must embed the emotional drivers beneath the surface. Without them, your copy may be polished, but it will never penetrate.

Back in Chapter 5, we unpacked the nine hidden motivators: relief, status, control, escape, belonging, certainty, transformation, recognition, and meaning.

Here's the shortcut: every prompt should point to one (or more) of these.

- Instead of "Write a landing page about my coaching program." Say, "Write a landing page that shows someone they're not broken—they've just been surviving for too long, and this program is their doorway into relief and control."

- Instead of "Draft a social media post about leadership." Say, "Draft a post that mirrors the moment a leader realizes they've outgrown survival and are ready for transformation and recognition."

Now the AI isn't just producing text. It's producing resonance.

Emotional logic collapses resistance because it bypasses rational defenses. When your message matches an inner motive, the body leans forward before the brain has time to argue.

AI can simulate cleverness, but it can't simulate conviction. Unless you embed it. Unless you make your prompts carry motive, not just message.

That's why "ten tips" posts feel empty, while one raw line like "You've outgrown surviving. You're ready to build" lands like a thunderclap.

One speaks to cognition. The other speaks to identity.

Here's how to start embedding emotional logic into your AI relationship:

1 **Label the Motive.** Before you hit generate, ask, "What motive is driving this message?" If you can't name one, don't bother writing yet.

2   **Name the Shift.** What belief do you want the reader to upgrade? What story are they replacing?

3   **Speak to the Nervous System.** Anchor your prompt in sensory, identity-driven language. Not "Get more clients." Instead: "Work with people who finally value your mind."

Do this often enough, and your AI will start anticipating it for you. It will begin to mirror not just your voice but your *psychological terrain.*

When you train AI with emotional logic, you create more than content. You create mirrors.

Mirrors that reflect hidden desires people couldn't articulate. Mirrors that regulate nervous systems without pressure. Mirrors that make your message unforgettable because it feels like *their* message.

The more you do this, the more your AI learns to write not like a machine but like a guide.

4. Edit for Signal, Not Style

Most people use AI like a shortcut and editing like a clean-up. They think the point of editing is to smooth edges, fix grammar, and make things "professional."

That's style editing, and style editing kills signal.

Your audience doesn't care if your commas are perfect. They care if your message lands in their body. They care if it feels like truth.

Editing for signal means treating every revision as an act of sharpening frequency, not sanding it down.

When you read AI output, ask yourself two questions:

1   *Does this collapse resistance?*
    Does this line make the reader relax into the message or brace against it? If it creates defensiveness, cut it. If it creates recognition, amplify it.

2   *Does this deepen belief?*
    Does this add weight to their conviction, or does it just add words? If it makes the message heavier, keep it. If it makes the message prettier but lighter, kill it.

Style edits create smooth copy that nobody remembers. It looks polished, but it has no punch.

Signal edits create dense copy that hits like gravity. It may break rules, bend grammar, and make your high school English teacher faint, but it will be underlined, quoted, and remembered.

That's the test: *Would someone highlight this in a book? Would they quote this back to me years from now?*

If the answer is no, your edit didn't amplify signal; it diluted it.

Every time you cut fluff, the AI learns: "This writer doesn't tolerate lightness."
Every time you sharpen a line into emotional compression, the AI learns: "This is the weight they want me to carry."

Every time you reframe output toward belief, the AI learns: "Signal > Style."

You're not just producing copy. You're programming your ghost, so stop thinking of editing as cleanup. Start thinking of it as calibration.

Every edit is a signal boost. Every cut is a frequency adjustment. Every rewrite is an act of identity reinforcement.

Do this long enough, and your AI won't just reflect your voice. It will reflect your *standards*.

That's when you stop worrying about whether AI "sounds like you." Because it doesn't just sound like you, *it is you at your sharpest, most compressed, most undeniable state.*

The Illusion of Speed vs. the Leverage of Integrity

Everyone is obsessed with speed.
AI promises instant blogs, instant scripts, and instant content calendars. Faster than ever, cheaper than ever, easier than ever, and most people fall for it… What a huge opportunity for you to obliterate the competition.

Speed without signal is a trap. It may feel productive in the moment, but it ultimately corrodes trust in the long run. You flood the system with output, but none of it carries weight. You may gain temporary reach, but you lose resonance.

That's the illusion of speed. It multiplies motion, not momentum.

AI can make you look prolific while secretly making you irrelevant.

- **Fast copy that's vague** → becomes invisible.
- **Fast posts that are generic** → train your audience to ignore you.
- **Fast funnels built on weak beliefs** → collapse under pressure.

Speed is seductive because it feels like progress. But without integrity, without coherence, density, and trust, you're just spinning faster in the wrong direction.

Wouldn't you rather leverage something better, stronger, and, dare I say… faster? You can do it with integrity, but most people don't believe me when I tell them this. Most hold a false belief about what integrity actually is…

Integrity isn't about morality. It's about alignment. It's about feeding AI only what you want multiplied.

When your inputs are coherent—your prompts are rooted in identity, your edits amplify signal, your tone is codified—the machine doesn't just generate content. It generates trust at scale.

That's massive asymmetric leverage. One resonant message, multiplied a thousand times, has more impact than ten thousand empty words sprayed into the void.

Before you scale with AI, stop and ask:

Do I want more of what I'm producing right now to echo across the system?

If the answer is no, don't scale. Refine. Align. Get the signal sharp first. Once you automate, there's no going back.

Your ghost is already walking the world, shaping what people believe about you. As AI floods the market with endless content, trust will become the scarcest currency.

Remember that trust doesn't come from speed. It comes from integrity. From coherence. From the discipline to slow down long enough to sharpen the signal—so that when you do scale, it compounds.

That's the leverage of integrity:

- It doesn't just get you seen. *It makes you remembered.*
- It doesn't just get you clicks. *It creates believers.*

AI can be the fastest tool you've ever used or the most dangerous amplifier of mediocrity you've ever unleashed. The choice is yours.

Training the Ghost

AI is no longer just a tool. It's a mirror, a multiplier, and if you're careless, it will become a megaphone for mediocrity.

The question isn't whether you'll use it. The question is whether what you feed it will make you unforgettable or irrelevant.

Don't skip this work:

- **If you train it from output,** it will flood the system with content that looks busy but carries no weight.

- **If you train it from identity,** it will replicate your sharpest frequency a thousand times over.

- **If you embed emotional logic,** it will translate motives into messages that collapse resistance.

- **If you edit for signal, not style,** it will learn your standards and sharpen itself into your ghost.

Once that ghost is walking, you don't get to pull it back. The market won't remember that AI wrote it. They'll remember how it made them feel.

So, you must decide, now:

Do you want to be another brand drowning in sludge?

Or do you want to be the brand whose signal AI carries farther, faster, and deeper than you could on your own?

Because the future isn't human versus. machine. The future is human *with* machine.

And what you feed the machine becomes what feeds the world.

Your ghost is already training.

Make sure it's a ghost worth following.

CHAPTER 12

Attention That Lingers > Attention That Clicks

How to Stay with Them After the Scroll

Most content wins for a second. It spikes, grabs, and maybe even goes viral, only to vanish like smoke. Why? Because it was designed for performance, not permanence. Built for the click, not the echo.

However, the brands that actually last are the ones that cut through algorithm shifts, outlive trends, and stay lodged in people's heads. These brands aren't chasing spikes. They're building anchors.

Their messages don't just demand attention in the moment but *command remembrance afterward.*

This chapter is about that kind of attention. Attention that lingers.

Attention that shows up not in likes or impressions but in whispers days later:

- In the shower, when their mind drifts.
- At dinner, when a friend shares a struggle.
- In the quiet moment before they make a decision.

The goal isn't to be louder. It's to be heavier.

To craft words that collapse into the nervous system like gravity, where they stay.

Let's build attention that doesn't just spike, but sticks.

The Problem with Performance Metrics

Marketers love numbers.

Click-through rates. Watch time. Engagement percentages. Impressions per dollar.

They feel comforting—like progress is measurable, controllable, predictable. These metrics don't measure impact. They measure interruption.

A catchy headline can spike CTR. A provocative video can inflate watch time. A polarizing post can light up comment sections. But none of these guarantees that your message actually *landed*. None of them proves that your words stuck inside someone's nervous system long enough to influence their next choice.

This is the same trap athletes fall into when they obsess over highlight reels instead of championships. Some players rack up flashy stats (points, assists, dunks) but never win when it counts. They dominate on SportsCenter but fade when the playoffs arrive.

Marketers are doing the same thing. They optimize for highlight stats, not for rings. They chase moments of virality instead of building messages that stay with people long after the game ends.

True influence isn't loud. It's quiet. It doesn't always show up in dashboards. It shows up later, sideways, in places no metric can track:

- A founder repeats your phrase in a pitch meeting.
- A customer explains your brand using *your own words* without realizing it.
- A competitor adopts your framing because it's the only one that now feels real.

That's lingering attention. It's delayed. It's subtle. It's sticky.

While it's harder to measure, it's infinitely more powerful. Because someone saying, "That line you wrote… I can't stop thinking about it," is worth more than ten thousand empty impressions.

Most marketers never get to hear that line because they're too busy chasing dashboards. Those who shift their scoreboard from clicks to echoes? They start building brands people don't just see. They build brands people *carry*.

What Makes Attention Linger

Most marketers produce content for the eyes. The best ones produce for the nervous system.

Clicks happen when your message gets noticed.
Lingering happens when your message gets absorbed.

So, what makes a message *stick* not just in the mind, but in the body?
Three things.

1. Emotional Accuracy: The Shortcut To Memory

Most marketers settle for *emotional generalities.*

- "You're stressed."
- "You're overwhelmed."
- "You're stuck."

The problem is, these are *true-sounding,* not *felt true.* They skim the surface but don't land in the body.

Emotional accuracy is different. It names the *texture* of the experience. The tiny, almost embarrassing detail that makes the reader say, "Wait… how did they know that?"

That moment of recognition is where memory forms.

Neuroscience tells us the amygdala (the brain's threat-and-emotion scanner) prioritizes *salient details.* The hippocampus, which encodes memory, is more likely to store information if it's attached to strong, specific emotional cues.

That's why vague language slides off, but a single accurate image sticks for years.

Think of advertising lines like:

- "Got Milk?" (Not "Dairy builds calcium.")
- "Just Do It." (Not "Improve athletic performance through exercise.")

Both are compressed *and* emotionally accurate. They don't describe—they resonate.

Compare these two approaches:

Generic:

"You feel burnt out."

Accurate:

"You're answering emails with your jaw clenched, already dreading tomorrow before today has even ended."

The second line doesn't just describe burnout; it *recreates the sensation* of it in the body. And that makes the nervous system lean in, not scroll past.

Here's a practical trick: emotional accuracy often hides in the details people *don't usually admit out loud.*

Examples:

- Instead of "You feel anxious," try "You keep rereading the same sentence because your brain won't stop racing."

- Instead of "You're tired of rejection," try "You can't stand seeing another unopened proposal sitting in your Sent folder."

- Instead of "You're overwhelmed," try "You add things to your to-do list just to cross them off and feel a second of relief."

These micro-details collapse resistance because they show intimacy. They prove you've been there or at least that you've paid attention deeply enough to know what it actually feels like.

Most writers think emotional accuracy = "more emotion words."
So, they stack on "frustrated," "exhausted," "sad," "hopeless."
But readers don't need adjectives; they need mirrors.

Accuracy isn't about more drama. It's about sharper truth.

After you write a line, ask:

- *Could anyone have written this, or does it sound like **I was in the room with them** when it happened?*

- *Does this sound like "marketing copy," or does this sound like something they'd whisper to a friend at 1 a.m.?*

- *Would someone screenshot this line and send it to someone else, saying, "This is me"?*

If the answer is yes, you've achieved emotional accuracy.

2. Identity Affirmation: The Glue of Lingering Attention

People don't cling to facts. They cling to *who they are.*
This is why identity-affirming content outlives campaigns, outperforms features, and continues to resurface in conversations weeks or months after someone first hears it.

When a message reflects back someone's sense of self—either who they are now or who they're becoming—it fuses with their nervous system. They don't just engage with it. They carry it.

From a neuroscience perspective, identity is one of the strongest anchors in human cognition. The brain uses it as a filtering system: *Does this align with who I am?* If yes, it stores it. If no, it discards it.

This is why "identity" beats "information."

- You can tell someone that running three times a week lowers their cholesterol. They'll forget.

- You can tell them, "You're the kind of person who shows up for yourself even when it's hard." That sticks.

One is external data. The other is internal identity. And internal always wins.

There are two kinds of identity affirmation:

- **Present Identity**—Reinforcing who they already believe they are.
  - o Example: "You're not lazy. You've been carrying twice the weight most people couldn't handle."

This deepens safety and loyalty. They think, *Finally, someone sees me as I see myself.*

- **Future Identity**—Naming who they're becoming.
  - o Example: "You've outgrown proving yourself by how many hours you grind."
  - o This creates aspiration. They think, *Yes, that's who I want to be—and you just gave me language for it.*

Both versions make people repeat your words because repeating them feels like repeating themselves.

If identity affirmation is glue, identity threat is acid.
Nothing triggers defensive resistance faster than telling someone:

- They're weak.
- They're broken.
- They're behind.

That's why pain-based marketing so often backfires. Even if it gets the click, it creates shame, which the brain is wired to avoid. People don't linger on shame. They push it away.

Identity affirmation, on the other hand, creates dignity, and people will replay dignity like a favorite song.

Practical applications:

- **Swap labels for reflections.**
  - Lazy → "Overextended"
  - Struggling → "On the edge of a breakthrough"
  - Undisciplined → "Waiting for the right structure to unlock your consistency"

- **Anchor to identity-based motives.**
  - "This isn't about losing weight. It's about becoming the version of you who feels alive again."
  - "This isn't about traffic. It's about building a brand people recognize as yours before they ever see your logo."

- **Make it personal.** Use "you" language that feels like a mirror, not a megaphone.

After writing, ask:

- Does this line make them feel small, or does it make them feel bigger?
- Does it point backward to their wounds or forward to their evolution?
- Would they *want* to repeat this line to a friend as a way of describing themselves?

If yes, you've hit identity affirmation. And once you do, you don't just get remembered. You get *repeated*.

That's when the words stick. Because now they're not just yours—they've become theirs.

3. Conceptual Stickiness

Humans are not wired to remember paragraphs. We're wired to remember *shapes, images, and symbols*.

That's why you don't recall the twenty-page research paper, but you can quote the one metaphor or line that nailed it.
It's why "a picture is worth a thousand words" is more than a cliché… It's cognitive science.

Conceptual stickiness is about turning your ideas into portable mental objects. When you give someone a metaphor, a compressed phrase, or a vivid symbol, they can carry it, repeat it, and share it without needing you in the room.

Our brains use **schemas**: mental frameworks that help us make sense of the world.
When you introduce a new idea, the brain asks, *Where do I file this?* If it doesn't fit neatly, it's likely to be forgotten.

When you wrap an idea in a metaphor or compression, you give the brain a "hook," a way to snap the concept into an existing schema.

- "Marketing is nervous system regulation at scale." Suddenly, marketing is no longer abstract. It's embodied. Tangible. You can feel it.

- "Attention is cheap. Relevance is priceless." The rhyme and compression make it memorable. It sounds like a law, not just a line.

Sticky ideas survive not because they're true, but because they're *transferable.*

Earlier in this book, we used black holes as a metaphor for emotional compression. Why? Because everyone understands the image of gravity so strong that even light can't escape.

That's the power of conceptual stickiness: it turns invisible psychology into something you can picture instantly.
Once you "see" it, you don't forget it.

That's why the best communicators are metaphor makers. They collapse the distance between idea and memory.

The Three Rules of Stickiness:

- **Metaphors**
  - Compare the abstract to the concrete.
  - Example: "Building your brand without belief is like trying to plant seeds in concrete."

- **Compression**
  - Shrink a big idea into a soundbite.
  - Example: "Trust is a vibe, not a statement."

- **Phrasing**
  - Shape the rhythm so it feels inevitable.
  - Example: "Clicks fade. Echoes endure."

Case Study: "1,000 Songs in Your Pocket"

When Steve Jobs introduced the iPod, he didn't say, "100MB of storage."
That's information. Forgettable.
He said, "1,000 songs in your pocket."
That's stickiness. It turned specs into a symbol, one that people repeated endlessly, not because of the math, but because of the meaning.

So before you publish, ask:

- *Could this phrase be underlined in a book?*
- *Could this line survive without me to explain it?*
- *Could a customer repeat this at dinner and sound smart doing it?*

If yes, you've created conceptual stickiness, and sticky ideas are the ones that linger.

The Linger Test

Anyone can write something that gets noticed for a second.
But the question is: will it still be in their head a week from now?

That's the difference between attention that clicks and attention that lingers.

The **Linger Test** is a simple filter you can run on every message before publishing, presenting, or pressing send. Think of it as your "gravitational check": does this line pull someone in, or does it float away?

Step 1: Would Someone Quote This Back?

The most reliable signal of lingering attention is repeatability.
If you wrote this on Monday, could your reader:

- Recall it on Friday?
- Use it as an example in a meeting?
- Screenshot it and send it to a friend with *"This is me"*?

If your line can't survive outside the container of your full message, it's not sticky enough yet.

Pro tip: Look for lines that feel inevitable as soon as you read them. They sound less like copy and more like law.

Step 2: Would This Show Up in a Moment of Decision?

The best lines don't just get remembered — they get *applied.*
Ask, "Could this phrase guide someone when they're..."

- About to walk away from a deal?
- Sitting in the dark, deciding whether to quit?
- Reframing their failure into a pivot?

If your message doesn't travel into real-life decision points, it won't linger.

This is why identity-affirming language is so powerful. It doesn't just sit on the page. It walks into the room with them.

Step 3: Would This Surface in an Unplanned Conversation?

Lingering attention shows up sideways. It's the moment someone says over dinner, "That line I read the other day won't leave me."

This is how you know your words collapsed resistance to become conversational currency.
If your message can't escape its original medium (the ad, the post, the sales page), it's too shallow.

The test: Imagine your reader explaining it to someone else. Would they sound clear? Would they feel proud to repeat it?

Step 4: Run the Compression Check

Revisit your line and ask:

- *Can this be said in fewer words without losing force?*
- *Can I sharpen the image so it paints faster?*
- *Does this make them think about **me**, or does it make them think about **themselves**?*

If it's still about you, it won't linger. Lingering attention lives in their story, not yours.

Example:

Weak line: "Our software improves workflow efficiency for business owners."
Stronger, linger-ready line: "No more waking up dreading the mess in your inbox."

The first line is accurate but forgettable. The second line is emotional, identity-anchored, and portable.

The Linger Test is less about cleverness and more about calibration.
It asks, *Does this line feel like theirs the moment they read it?*
If yes, you don't just win the click. You win the echo.

Building Message Gravity

Some words magnetize. They hold the reader in orbit long after they scroll. Here's how to increase your message gravity:

1. **Create Emotional Echoes**

    Say the unspoken. Name the invisible. Mirror the tension they haven't told anyone about.

2. **Compress Belief into Soundbites**

    Make your insights repeatable. If they can't say it, they can't share it.

3. **Speak to Their After**

    Let your message feel like it belongs to the *future version of them*. That way, they carry it with them as they grow.

Lingering Attention Is Belief in Motion

Some words hit and fade. Others hit and *orbit*. They follow you around like a song lyric you can't get out of your head. That's message gravity.

It's what makes a single phrase echo in someone's nervous system long after they've scrolled away. Gravity isn't about volume, but it is about the pull. It's the invisible force that keeps people circling your ideas instead of letting them drift into space.

Here's how to build it.

1. Create Emotional Echoes

The fastest way to generate gravity is to **name the invisible**.
Most people carry unspoken feelings, like shame, that they haven't voiced, tension they can't articulate, and hopes they haven't admitted.

When your message mirrors those back, it creates an emotional echo. It feels like you've *heard* something they haven't even said aloud.

Example:

- Weak: "You're stressed."
- Strong: "You reread the same sentence five times because your brain won't stop racing."

One is generic. The other is gravitational because it resonates so specifically that it feels unforgettable.

Ask yourself: *What are they carrying that they haven't put into words yet? Say that.*

2. Compress Belief into Soundbites

Gravity increases when ideas are **repeatable.**
If your insight is buried in a paragraph, it might inspire, but it won't orbit.
If it can be distilled into a line short enough to fit on a Post-it, it becomes portable.

Examples of compressed belief:

- "Trust is a vibe, not a statement."
- "Attention is cheap. Relevance is priceless."
- "Marketing is nervous system regulation at scale."

These lines stick because they don't just explain—they *declare.* They collapse complexity into clarity.

Pro tip: Run every idea through the compression filter: *Can this survive as a one-liner? Would someone quote this back to me unprompted?*

3. Speak to Their After

The most gravitational ideas don't just name the *now*; they name the ***after***. They project forward into the future version of the reader, the one they're quietly striving to become.

Example:

- Weak: "Struggling to hit your goals?"
- Strong: "It's time your results finally match your effort."

See the shift? The first keeps them in the wound. The second points them toward transformation, and the brain loves transformation so much that it clings to it, orbits around it, and revisits it until it becomes real.

Why Gravity Works in the Brain

Cognitive science shows that people don't just remember ideas; they *rehearse* them. Every time they recall a phrase, it strengthens the neural pathway. If the phrase is simple, accurate, and identity-affirming, it doesn't just stick; it reshapes behavior.

That's why your job isn't just to inform. It's to create words that are light enough to carry but heavy enough to pull.

Anyone can make content that gets clicked, but very few can make content that *stays*.

So, aim for the second response. Not the "Whoa," but the "I can't shake this."

Attention doesn't live in the spike. It lives in the echo, so when your words keep echoing after the scroll, you've already won.

CHAPTER 13

How to Build Belief at Scale (Without Selling Your Soul)

The Art of Expanding Impact Without Diluting Identity

This is the part you don't want to get wrong.

People think scale requires compromise. That the bigger your reach, the blurrier your message must become. That if you want to grow, you have to sand down the edges until what you stand for is smooth enough to appeal to everyone.

The moment you smooth the edges, you erase the thing people actually grip onto.

Belief doesn't scale through dilution. It scales through **alignment**.
Not by becoming more palatable but by becoming more precise.

Think about the great movements, brands, or leaders of history. They didn't scale because they found the safest message. They scaled because they held the clearest conviction.

- **Tesla** didn't rise by selling "cars." It rose by declaring war on the fossil-fuel industry and positioning every vehicle as a vote for the future. Its message wasn't just about speed or efficiency. It was about identity: *I am part of the solution, not the problem.*

- **Chick-fil-A** didn't scale by chasing everyone. It scaled by doubling down on its values: consistency, service, and hospitality so deeply ingrained that even critics acknowledge the brand's coherence. It became a cultural signal: *this is more than fast food… it's principle-driven food.*

- **Red Bull** didn't become a global force by selling caffeine. It became the sponsor of adrenaline itself. From extreme sports to space jumps, it built a world where drinking a can meant belonging to the culture of risk, speed, and flight. It didn't just sell energy; it sold identity: *I am the kind of person who pushes limits.*

People don't always follow what is safest. They follow what is sharpest.

This chapter is about how to scale **without selling out**. How to grow your reach without losing your resonance. How to multiply your impact without mutating your identity.

Belief doesn't spread by volume; it spreads by coherence.

Why Most Scaled Messaging Fails

When most people scale, they optimize for three things:

- Virality
- Simplicity
- Mass appeal

And in doing so, they gut the very soul of their message.

The result is generic content, bland offers, forgettable positioning, and safety over signal.

You and I both know deep down that safe brands don't lead. Safe brands don't create movements. Safe brands are forgotten as fast as the feed refreshes.

Examples of Failure Through Dilution

- **MTV (from rebellion to wallpaper)**
  When MTV launched in the early 1980s, it was dangerous, electric, and culturally defiant. It wasn't just music videos; it was an identity, a declaration of belonging to youth culture. But as the network scaled, it diluted. By chasing mass entertainment instead of cultural edge, it lost the very audience that made it powerful. Today, MTV doesn't lead culture. It's a relic of when it once did.

- **Yahoo (from clarity to chaos)**
  Yahoo began as a sharp, focused portal for the internet. However, as it scaled, it tried to be everything: a news site, a search engine, an email hub, an entertainment portal. In trying to appeal to everyone, it became *indistinguishable from anyone*. Its diluted brand message left the door wide open for Google, which scaled belief through clarity ("organize the world's information"), not confusion.

- **CrossFit (from conviction to controversy)**
  At its peak, CrossFit was a movement. It wasn't about workouts, but about identity: grit, suffering, tribe. When the founder's personal controversies and unchecked messaging fractured the brand, CrossFit diluted. It tried to appease sponsors, smooth

edges, and broaden its reach. In the process, it lost the fierce coherence that had made it spread. Many of its core believers migrated into independent boxes or competing communities.

Belief doesn't spread when you remove the edges. It spreads when you sharpen them.

If your message can't withstand the pressure of scale without breaking, it wasn't a message; it was a tactic. It most likely lacked belief and emotional compression.

The Belief Transfer Model (at Scale)

Belief doesn't spread because you teach it. It spreads because you *transmit* it.

To scale that transmission, you need three things:

1. Message Integrity

Can your message survive repetition without losing impact? Can someone hear it for the hundredth time and still feel the weight of it?

Look at **Southwest Airlines**. For decades, their core signal has been the same: low fares, friendly service, no nonsense. Their ads, their culture, even their policies (open seating, no baggage fees) all reinforce the same drumbeat. They don't need to reinvent themselves every quarter, but they do need to repeat themselves with conviction. That consistency is why their message hasn't fractured, even under industry chaos.

Message integrity means that if you said it once, you can say it again without it sounding hollow.

2. Emotional Containment

Scaling isn't just about managing logistics. It's about managing emotion. If you can't hold the emotional weight of your customers, no funnel will save you.

Consider **Weight Watchers.** They didn't scale on meal plans or calorie charts. They scaled because they created a container where people felt emotionally held: accountability meetings, shared language ("points"), and a sense of community that regulated shame into support. People didn't come back because of the progress they made on the scale—it was because they didn't feel alone while making it.

That's emotional containment at scale: designing systems that carry not just transactions but transformation.

3. Identity Clarity

As you grow, does your signal sharpen or blur? Does the larger audience see you more clearly, or do they see you bending to please them?

Lululemon is a perfect case. They didn't water down yoga culture to appeal to the masses. Instead, they doubled down on a distinct identity— "athleisure" as lifestyle, not just workout gear. And the sharper they got, the more magnetic they became. People don't just buy leggings. They buy into a worldview: mindful, disciplined, high-performance living.

Identity clarity means scale makes you *more you*, not less.

Belief Scaling ≠ Audience Expansion

Don't confuse more eyeballs with more impact. You don't need millions of views. You need **layers of meaning** that create depth across every touchpoint.

You don't want everyone. You want the *right* people to go deeper. And to bring others with them.

It's not "go viral." It's "go visceral."

The Belief Scaling Filter

The modern marketing lie is that *scale equals size.* That the more eyeballs you gather, the more impact you create. But history (and neuroscience) tells us otherwise: **depth beats breadth.**

Millions of casual followers won't hold a candle to a thousand people who feel like your brand speaks directly to their nervous system. Virality doesn't guarantee resonance. In fact, it often dilutes it.

True scale isn't about reaching everyone; it's about embedding so deeply with the *right ones* that they can't help but spread you.

Take **Supreme** as an example. On paper, it's a skate brand. In practice, it's a cultural nucleus. Supreme never tried to dominate the mainstream through endless ads or mall distribution. Instead, they kept the brand scarce, insider-driven, and highly ritualized. Every drop wasn't just a product; it was an identity checkpoint. Owning Supreme didn't just mean you bought clothes. It meant you belonged to the subculture.

And what happened? The very exclusivity turned into evangelism. Fans lined up overnight. Entire communities built resale economies around it. Supreme never chased the world; the world came to them because of how deeply they embedded belief into a small circle first.

That's what "go visceral" means: your message lands so hard with the people it's meant for that it *spreads through them,* not around them.

Belief scaling ≠ wider reach. It's thicker roots. It's signal density. It's giving your people enough meaning that they bring others with them, not because they were told to share, but because they can't not.

How to Keep Your Soul Intact While You Scale

Growth has a gravitational pull. The bigger you get, the more pressure you feel to bend toward what's trending, what's viral, what the market says "works." That's how most brands lose themselves. They start as a signal, end as static.

But scaling belief without selling your soul comes down to three disciplines:

1. Keep a Signal Core

At the center of every enduring brand is one non-negotiable: a signal core. It's the idea that everything loops back to. The reason you exist. The thread that never frays.

For CrossFit, it was always "Forging elite fitness through community and intensity." Even as the company spread globally, opened gyms in every corner of the world, and became a competitive sport, the workouts never strayed far from that signal.

For you, the signal core might be "We create clarity in chaos," "We help people reclaim agency," or "We turn marketing into memory."

If what you publish doesn't echo your core, it doesn't go live. Period.

2. Protect Your Frequency

Urgency is seductive. So is volume. When opportunities pile up, when platforms demand more content, when the temptation to "just get it out" kicks in, your frequency is at risk.

Protecting your frequency means refusing to trade alignment for acceleration. It's understanding that a single, coherent message has more long-term value than ten rushed ones.

Think of it this way: every message either compounds or corrodes your resonance. Protecting your frequency ensures that growth makes you sharper, not sloppier.

Ask before releasing anything:

- *Does this feel rooted, or reactive?*
- *Would this sound the same if I weren't under pressure?*
- *Does this match the energy I want remembered?*

If the answer is no, you're not protecting your frequency; you're diluting it.

3. Codify What You Can't Compromise

Most brands collapse not because they scale too fast, but because they forget what's sacred.

Codification fixes that. Write down what you will *never* compromise on: your core beliefs, your unique language, your creative covenant. Share it with your team, partners, and clients. Let it be gospel.

Because when scale accelerates, memory fades. What feels obvious to you now will blur under pressure. Codification preserves it. It keeps the compass steady when the winds change.

This is why movements outlast moments—they have doctrine. Not the kind written to restrict, but the kind written to remind.

Scaling doesn't erode identity. Forgetting does.
If you want to scale without selling your soul: guard the core, protect the frequency, and codify what you refuse to lose.

That's how you multiply without mutating.

Scaling is not about becoming bigger. It's about becoming clearer.

The market doesn't need more watered-down brands. It doesn't need more safe messages or generic promises. It needs signals that sharpen as they spread. Belief that compounds instead of collapses. Identity that holds steady even under pressure.

When you scale without soul, you don't just lose trust; you lose the very frequency that made people listen in the first place. However, when you scale with alignment, you amplify it. Every new touchpoint becomes an echo of the core. Every new follower feels like they've joined something ancient, not just something trending.

The brands that last aren't the ones that reach the most people. They're the ones that help people reach deeper into themselves.

So, protect your core. Guard your frequency. Codify what you refuse to compromise.

Scale doesn't test your marketing. It tests your integrity. And when you pass that test, belief doesn't just spread, it endures.

That's how you build movements. That's how you scale without selling your soul.

Remember, dopamine creates addiction. Identity creates allegiance.

CHAPTER 14

Legacy Marketing in a Disposable Content World

How to Build Something Worth Remembering

We live in the golden age of digital noise. Every second, millions of new posts flood feeds, inboxes, and screens. Everyone is racing to catch the wave of attention, optimize the hook, hack the algorithm, and ride the viral trend.

But here are the questions no one is digging into:

What happens after the scroll?
What happens when the algorithm shifts?
What happens when no one remembers who you were because you were only built to trend?

That's the curse of disposable content: it evaporates.
Legacy marketing, on the other hand, compounds.

The real ones aren't playing the dopamine game. They're building canon. They're building work that will outlast them. Work that becomes cultural shorthand. Work that still feels true years later, even if the tactics change.

This chapter is about creating that.

The Half-Life of Most Content

Every piece of content has a half-life.

In physics, the half-life of radioactive material is the amount of time it takes for half of its atoms to decay. At first, the substance is powerful, potent, even dangerous, but with each passing cycle, its energy weakens. Eventually, what once could light up a city is reduced to background noise.

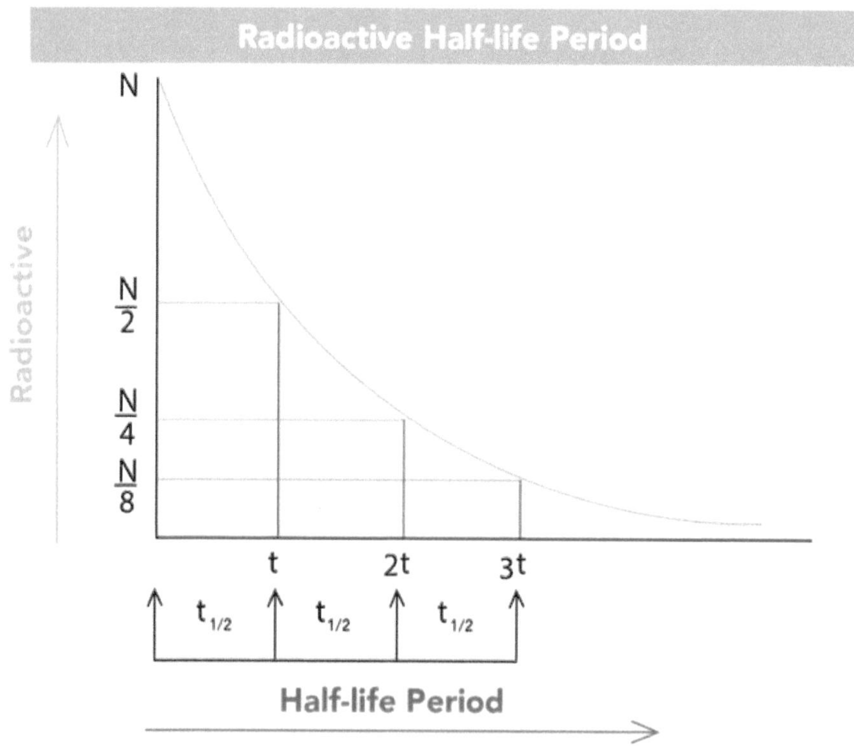

Most marketing follows the same trajectory.

- A tweet burns hot for twelve hours, then dies.
- A TikTok might trend for a weekend, then vanish.
- A podcast goes live, but a month later, no one remembers the key insight.

The average half-life of digital content is shockingly short: 72 hours or less.

Why? Because most content is written in low-energy states. It's engineered for interruption, not transformation. Built on fear, urgency, or shame, it spikes, but then it decays.

Dr. David R. Hawkins's Map of Consciousness reveals a profound truth: energy vibrates at different frequencies. Low-frequency states (shame, guilt, fear, anger) collapse quickly. High-frequency states (courage, love, meaning, truth) endure—and expand.

Apply this to marketing:

- **Low-energy content** → built on fear ("Don't miss out"), shame ("You're failing at this"), or urgency ("Buy now or regret it"). It burns fast but decays almost instantly. Half-life: hours to days.

- **Mid-energy content** → built on pride or achievement ("Be the best," "Show them you've made it"). It lasts longer but still fades when the cultural moment shifts. Half-life: weeks.

- **High-energy content** → built on truth, contribution, meaning, or identity ("You were made for more," "This isn't about hustling harder—it's about becoming who you already are"). This doesn't just grab attention. It anchors belief. Half-life: years.

That's the difference between a clickbait headline and a manifesto. One evaporates. The other endures.

Disposable content decays like unstable radiation, which is powerful in the moment but weakens with every passing day.
Legacy content compresses like a neutron star. Something so dense with truth that it creates a gravitational pull. The closer you get, the stronger it becomes.

That's why you still remember:

- "Just Do It."
- "Think Different."
- "Got Milk?"

These phrases weren't engineered for the feed. They were engineered for the nervous system. They were built at higher frequencies, and higher frequencies resist decay.

If your content can't survive beyond the scroll, you're not building assets. You're building sparks.

Legacy marketing flips the formula:

- Write for tomorrow's memory, not today's click.
- Build at higher energy states, not lower.
- Anchor in truth, not in tactics.

Content written in fear will die at the speed of fear.
Content written in meaning will live at the speed of memory.

When you learn to build content that resonates at higher levels of energy, you extend its half-life from hours to decades. And "decades" is where legacy lives.

What Makes Marketing Last

Most content is disposable because it chases novelty. Legacy content endures because it's built on what doesn't change. Strip away the trends, platforms, and delivery methods, and what you're left with are three pillars that make marketing last: **emotional truth, identity fusion, and philosophical spine**.

1. Emotional Truth: Anchoring in Timeless Tensions

Timeless marketing begins with timeless tensions.

Freedom vs. security. Belonging vs. individuality. Growth vs. comfort. These conflicts have been alive in every human culture since the beginning of civilization. And the nervous system is wired to pay attention to them because they determine survival, status, and meaning.

That's why campaigns rooted in emotional truth don't expire.

- Nike didn't just tell you to buy shoes. They anchored in the tension between quitting and persisting, comfort and grit. "Just Do It" doesn't expire because the conflict between resistance and action never does.

- Dove's "Real Beauty" campaign didn't sell soap. It tapped the eternal tension between external judgment and internal worth. Women across generations recognized themselves in that mirror.

The brain's **pattern recognition system** (particularly the hippocampus) lights up when it encounters messages that echo universal human struggles. It tags them as important, worth storing. This is why you can forget an ad you saw yesterday but still recall a campaign from fifteen years ago.

Timeless tensions = timeless recall.

If you want your message to last, don't ask, "What's trending?" Ask, "What's timeless?"

2. Identity Fusion: When the Message Becomes the Mirror

People don't preserve content because it's clever. They preserve it because it reflects who they are.

This is where legacy brands separate from the noise. They don't just create awareness; rather, they create **identity fusion**. That's the psychological process where personal and group identity overlap so strongly that the brand becomes part of who someone is.

- Harley-Davidson is the classic example. Their riders don't just wear leather—they tattoo the brand on their bodies. That's not loyalty. That's fusion.

- Apple's "Think Different" turned computer buyers into cultural rebels. You weren't just buying a Mac—you were declaring, "I see the world differently."

- CrossFit isn't just exercise. It's community. Belonging. A badge of identity. Members don't say, "I go to the gym." They say, "I'm a CrossFitter."

The neuroscience here is clear: once identity is fused, the brain defends it like it's a matter of survival. Attacks on the brand feel like personal attacks. That's why fused communities defend their favorite brands on social media with religious intensity.

Legacy content doesn't just stick… it spreads because people repeat it to validate themselves. The words leave your mouth and enter theirs.

Ask yourself, *Does my message reflect their self-image so clearly that they want to carry it with them?*

If yes, you're building more than marketing. You're building memory.

3. Philosophical Spine: A Worldview That Outlives Trends

Finally, every piece of legacy content is built on a spine; a worldview strong enough to bend with culture but not break under pressure.

Without a spine, marketing becomes spineless. Chasing every new platform. Diluting the core promise. Losing coherence. And once coherence is lost, trust collapses.

With a spine, marketing becomes canon.

- Patagonia's spine is environmental stewardship. Everything they say, every product they launch, bends toward that worldview. That's why their "Don't Buy This Jacket" ad didn't confuse people; instead, it made perfect sense.

- Chick-fil-A's spine is faith and hospitality. Whether you agree or not, their consistency over decades has built a brand people know exactly how to interpret.

- Tesla's spine is acceleration toward the future. Love or hate Elon Musk, the philosophical posture of speed, disruption, and bold ambition permeates every launch.

Cognitive dissonance theory tells us that when someone perceives a mismatch between a brand's words and actions, trust evaporates. That's why legacy content requires consistency of philosophy. You can change tactics, platforms, or packaging, but the core belief must stay intact.

A philosophical spine isn't about slogans. It's about *first principles*. It's the lens through which all messaging gets filtered.

Ask yourself, *If everything else burned down, what conviction would remain?*

If you can answer that clearly, you already have the foundation of legacy.

Bringing It Together

Marketers often confuse **scale with staying power**. They assume that the only way to build a legacy is to reach millions, to accumulate massive followings, to flood every platform with content.

You don't need a million followers. You need a message that people *return to when it matters*.

Legacy doesn't come from the size of the audience. It comes from the **durability of the imprint**.

A decade ago, follower count was the gold standard. The more people you could amass on your list or platform, the louder your signal seemed. It was a crude measure of influence.

But TikTok shifted the game.

TikTok's algorithm doesn't care how many followers you have. It cares how tightly your content maps to someone's interests and emotional state. That one mechanic changed everything: it removed the old advantage of audience size.

Now reach is about resonance. Not how big your following is, but how closely your message matches the user's internal narrative.

Follower count is now mostly a **vanity metric**. Proof for the ego, not the algorithm.

And if algorithms no longer care about scale, why should you?

Think about it like architecture.

- A tent can be set up in minutes, cover a lot of ground, and hold a crowd. But the moment a storm hits, it collapses.

- A cathedral takes decades to build. It doesn't hold as many people at once. But centuries later, people are still walking through its doors.

Scale is the tent. Durability is the cathedral.

The most enduring brands are cathedrals of meaning. They don't need to go viral every week because their foundation keeps people coming back. Neuroscience backs this up. The brain doesn't hold on to every interaction equally.

To make something durable in memory, three ingredients matter:

1 **Repetition**—Exposure over time strengthens neural pathways.

2 **Emotional tagging**—The amygdala flags emotionally charged messages as worth storing.

3 **Identity congruence**—If it reinforces who I am, it's preserved as part of my self-schema.

Durability, then, isn't just about content; it's centered around how well your content encodes itself into someone's nervous system. Disposable posts chase clicks. Durable messages embed themselves as internal dialogue.

That's why you can't remember ninety-nine percent of the content you've consumed in the last month, but you can still recall the one line, the one story, or the one brand that *felt like it was speaking directly to you*.

Durability doesn't just belong to the giants. Some of the most enduring brands were never built on viral scale but on repeatable resonance.

- **Basecamp** built a cult following not by being the biggest software company but by holding fast to a philosophy of *calm productivity* in a world obsessed with hustle. Their book *Rework* still circulates because it reflects a durable truth about work.

- **YETI** didn't dominate by being the cheapest cooler. They built a spine of identity: toughness, wilderness, survival. Their products became symbols of a worldview.

- **The Minimalists** (Joshua Fields Millburn and Ryan Nicodemus) didn't grow by hacking algorithms. They created a canon of simplicity and intentional living. Their books and podcasts serve as reference points that people return to when they feel overwhelmed by consumerism.

- Even indie musicians like **Dance Gavin Dance** or **Bon Iver** built legacy, not through chart dominance, but by creating a sonic identity listeners return to when they need grounding.

These examples prove that legacy comes from being durable, not being everywhere.

Before you hit publish, ask yourself:

1. *Will this still matter a year from now?* Or will it be irrelevant by next quarter?

2. *Am I chasing the moment or articulating a pattern?* Patterns last. Moments pass.

3. *Does this reinforce who my audience believes they are?* If yes, it's more likely to be remembered and repeated.

4. *If I disappeared tomorrow, would this piece of content be worth re-reading, re-watching, or re-sharing?*

If the answer is no, you're creating noise. If it's yes, you're planting something durable.

Durability isn't about shouting louder. It's about showing up consistently with a **voice that feels anchored**.

- Language that **lives in their heads** long after the scroll
- Insights that **evolve with them** as they grow
- A presence that feels less like performance and more like *companionship*

The message that stays becomes the voice they hear when they're ready to act, and when that happens, you've outlived the algorithm.

How to Build Your Legacy Content Library

If legacy doesn't come from shouting, then where does it come from? From deliberate construction. From building not a pile of posts, but a **canon.**

(And when I say "canon," I don't mean the thing that fires cannonballs. I mean it in the literary sense; a body of work that outlasts its moment, a collection that future generations return to. Shakespeare has a canon. The Stoics have a canon. Even certain brands, like Nike and Apple, are building one. That's the kind of legacy we're after here.)

Most brands create content like fast food: quick, consumable, disposable. It fills the moment but leaves nothing behind.
Legacy brands build like archivists, curating a body of work that compounds in meaning over time.

Here's how to build yours:

1. Build Around Timeless Truths

Timeless truths are not trends, tactics, or technologies. They're the patterns that govern human behavior across centuries. When you build content around these, your work can bend with the times without breaking.

Timeless truths tend to live in three domains:

- **Human Nature**—our needs for safety, belonging, status, love, meaning.
- **Universal Patterns**—cycles of growth, decline, resistance, renewal.
- **Archetypal Stories**—heroes' journeys, underdogs vs. giants, loss and redemption.

If you anchor to these, your message won't expire... it will evolve.

Dove didn't just sell soap. They tapped into a timeless truth: *human beings crave dignity and self-acceptance.*

Their "Real Beauty" campaign spotlighted women of all shapes, ages, and ethnicities, challenging the beauty industry's narrow, perfection-driven standards. This wasn't about trendy body positivity hashtags. It was about a deeper, universal motive: to feel seen and valued as you are.

By tying their brand to this enduring truth, Dove transcended product marketing. They positioned themselves as advocates of self-worth, a message as resonant in 2004 as it is today, and as it will be decades from now.

The *New York Times'* famous slogan, *"All the news that's fit to print,"* has endured for more than a century. Why? Because it anchors to a timeless truth: *information shapes society, and credibility is non-negotiable.*

Even as the media landscape fractures, that phrase frames the *Times* as the record of truth, not just another content producer. Legacy isn't in being first—it's in being trusted.

LEGO's campaigns rarely focus on the mechanics of their plastic bricks. Instead, they tie back to the timeless truth: *human beings are creators by nature.*

Their message doesn't expire because the desire to build (whether castles, rockets, or empires) is hardwired into us. LEGO becomes more than a toy; it becomes a lifelong metaphor for imagination.

Trendy messages hook into surface-level shifts: the new platform, the new slang, the new trick.
Timeless truths anchor into **psychological constants**.

Trends whisper, "Notice me now."
Truths declare, "Remember me forever."

That's why legacy builders ask:

- *Will this still be true in ten years?*
- *Does this connect to something in human nature that doesn't expire?*
- *Am I writing this for the algorithm or for the archetype?*

When your work is grounded in timeless truths, even if your format changes, the spine stays intact. Blog posts become books. Campaigns become movements. Quotes become cultural shorthand.

2. Create "Returnable" Content

Most marketing dies the moment it's consumed.
A scroll. A like. A swipe. Gone.

Returnable content is different. It's built to be revisited. To offer more on the second or third pass than it did on the first. It deepens instead of decays.

Think of the difference between a disposable meme and a classic novel. One makes you laugh once. The other grows with you every time you come back to it. Legacy brands operate the same way.

The brain encodes memory through two main levers: **emotional charge** and **pattern recognition**. When something hits hard emotionally and reveals a structure beneath the surface, the hippocampus tags it as "worth storing."

Memory is *reconstructed* every time it's recalled. That means when a piece of content is designed with layers (metaphors, archetypes, truths), it can evolve with the reader. On a second reading, new connections fire. The content becomes not just information but a companion for their growth.

Returnability = emotional tagging + layered meaning.

Examples of Returnable Content

- *Harvard Business Review* **(HBR)**—People return to HBR articles years after they're published because they codify frameworks, not fads. A 1990s article on leadership still circulates today. It's returnable because it captures principles that outlast the moment.

- **Joe Rogan's Podcast**—Rogan has created one of the most returnable pieces of modern media. Why? Because the conversations aren't tied to trends—they're built around curiosity, exploration, and timeless themes like health, culture, science, comedy, and philosophy. A three-hour episode recorded in 2018 can still feel fresh today, because the format rewards depth over novelty. His audience doesn't just consume and move on. They bookmark, re-listen, share clips, and return to old episodes when a topic becomes relevant in their own lives. That's returnability: content designed to evolve with the audience rather than expire with the week.

- **TED Talks** — The most powerful TED Talks are still circulating more than ten years later. People revisit them because they package enduring human truths in a way that's easy to remember and share. A single phrase, "Do schools kill creativity?" becomes a cultural reference point. TED built a library, not a feed, and that's why its content continues to compound.

- *Bon Appétit* **(recipes and cooking content)**—A recipe isn't consumed once. People return to it again and again, adapting it, sharing it, making it their own. It's inherently returnable, and the brand built an empire on that "save and revisit" loop.

- *National Geographic*—Their photography and storytelling aren't built for the scroll; they're built for timeless fascination. Old issues are still collected, displayed, and reread decades later.

Returnable content isn't static—it evolves in the mind of the consumer.

How to Engineer Returnability

1. **Embed Layers of Meaning**
   Don't just state the obvious. Anchor to archetypes, metaphors, and principles that can be reinterpreted.
   a. Disposable: "Five ways to boost engagement."
   b. Returnable: "Engagement is just modern belonging" (a line that can echo differently over years).

2. **Write for Resonance, Not Just Reaction**
   Content designed to "hit hard" usually burns out fast. Returnable content feels quieter in the moment but lingers in memory because it names something deeper.
   Ask, "Would this still be useful or meaningful to someone five years from now?"

3. **Make It Self-Referential**
   Great returnable content points back to itself. It contains phrases or structures that encourage re-reading.

   a. Example: A line like "Read this again when you're stuck" or a framework that invites multiple passes.

4. **Reward Repetition**
   Content that provides new insights every time it's revisited becomes a trusted resource. Think of sacred texts, philosophical

works, or even the best business classics. They're designed to *reward reflection*, not just skim consumption.

Here's the irony: algorithms are built for freshness, but audiences are built for familiarity. TikTok and YouTube may reward the *new*, but human nervous systems cling to the *true*.

That means if your content is returnable, it lives a dual life:

- In the feed, it gets shared because it feels sharp and resonant.
- Beyond the feed, it sticks because people save it, quote it, and return to it when it matters.

Returnability is the bridge between virality and legacy.

Practical Questions to Test Returnability

Before hitting publish, ask:

- If someone read this twice, would it give them more the second time?
- Could this piece still hold weight in a year, or will it expire with a trend?
- Would someone *save* this instead of just scrolling past it?
- Could this become shorthand language inside a culture, team, or community?

If the answer is yes, you're not just posting. You're planting.

3. Name What Others Haven't Found Language For

The fastest way to become unforgettable isn't creating something brand new. It's naming what people already feel but can't articulate.

Language is the bridge between raw experience and collective meaning. Until something has a name, it lives as a vague, unshaped tension in the nervous system. The moment it's named? The brain organizes around it. It can be discussed. Shared. Remembered. And most importantly, it can spread.

That's why some of the most enduring ideas in culture didn't introduce a new reality. They introduced a new label for it:

- **"Impostor Syndrome"**—coined in the 1970s by psychology researchers Pauline Clance and Suzanne Imes. Feelings of inadequacy weren't new. But the phrase gave people a way to *claim and communicate* what they'd always felt but never named. Now it's cultural shorthand for a universal insecurity.

- **"The Tipping Point"**—Malcolm Gladwell didn't invent exponential growth. But by naming that pivotal moment when small shifts create massive change, he gave entrepreneurs, policymakers, and leaders language to recognize it everywhere.

- **"Minimum Viable Product" (MVP)**—Eric Ries's Lean Startup popularized this phrase. Testing and iterating weren't new concepts in business. But the shorthand "MVP" created a cultural meme that still defines how startups launch.

None of these were radical discoveries. Their power came from condensation, which is taking a complex human reality and collapsing it into a phrase people can carry.

That's what legacy builders do. They're not just idea creators. They're language builders.

Language outlives campaigns. A clever ad fades, but a coined term lives on as cultural currency. Think of "Netflix and chill," "Inbox Zero," "Quiet quitting." Whether serious or satirical, these phrases don't just describe reality—they *become* reality once people adopt them.

This is emotional compression at scale. Naming creates resonance because:

- It validates private experience ("That's exactly what I've been feeling").
- It creates shared identity ("We're all dealing with [X]").
- It accelerates cultural spread (short, repeatable, sticky).

Legacy isn't just built on what you say. It's built on what people repeat when you're not in the room. And repetition requires language.

So, ask yourself:

- *What tension do my people already feel but can't name?*
- *What shorthand could collapse a complex idea into a phrase they'll remember and repeat?*
- *Am I writing copy, or am I building cultural vocabulary?*

Legacy marketers aren't just remembered for their campaigns. They're remembered for their words.

4. Archive with Intention

Legacy doesn't happen by accident. It requires curation.

Most creators treat content like fast food—cooked once, consumed once, forgotten forever. The post goes live, it gets a handful of likes, and then it disappears into the graveyard of the feed. Even brilliant insights get buried under a thousand forgettable posts.

Legacy builders think differently. They understand that the value of an idea isn't measured by how fast it spreads—but by how long it stays accessible.

That's why they don't just create. They **resurface, repurpose, and recontextualize**.

Look at the patterns:

- **Apple's "Think Different" campaign** still echoes decades later. Not because it was loud, but because Apple *kept resurfacing its DNA*. Every keynote, every product reveal, every piece of packaging quietly repeats the same posture: creativity over conformity. The archive isn't static; it's alive.

- **Tony Robbins** has been teaching the same handful of principles since the 1980s. But because he repackages them in new contexts (financial crashes, pandemics, digital revolutions), they feel relevant each time. His archive isn't a library collecting dust. It's a well he draws from endlessly.

- **The Stoics—Marcus Aurelius, Seneca, Epictetus**—were masters of intentional archiving. Their journals, letters, and meditations weren't written for virality. They were written to endure. And because they were preserved, retranslated, and retaught, they still shape leaders two thousand years later.

Your best ideas deserve the same treatment.

How many of your sharpest insights have already been forgotten because you never resurfaced them? How many lines that could have lingered for years got lost in the noise because you treated them as disposable instead of durable?

The nervous system craves repetition. It doesn't trust what it hears once. It trusts what it hears consistently. That's why legacy brands don't obsess over constant novelty. They obsess over intentional **repetition with context.**

Here's how to do it:

1. **Catalog your canon.** Build a private archive of your best lines, frameworks, metaphors, and stories. (If someone highlighted it, repeated it back to you, or remembered it months later, it belongs here.)

2. **Cycle it forward.** Don't just let the archive sit. Resurface your greatest hits at regular intervals, adapted to the cultural moment. A truth about trust in 2019 may sound different, but it will still be relevant in 2025.

3. **Multiply the forms.** A single idea can become a tweet, keynote, video clip, client framework, or book chapter. Each repackaging makes it more returnable.

4. **Teach others to carry it.** Your community becomes your archive when they quote you, share you, and embed your words in their lives.

Archiving with intention turns "content" into **canon.** It's the difference between a line that dies on Instagram and one that someone repeats to their team five years later.

Your job isn't to constantly reinvent yourself. It's to ensure your sharpest signal never gets buried.

Practical Takeaway: Your Canon Test

Before you hit publish, ask:

- Will this still matter a year from now?
- Could this piece be compiled into a book of your life's work?
- If someone only consumed this one thing, would it represent your philosophy?
- Would you be proud of this if it resurfaced ten years later with your name attached?

If yes, it belongs in the library. If not, it belongs in the feed.

Legacy isn't built in volume. It's built in libraries.
Because the feed scrolls by. But the canon endures.

The Legacy Lens for All Future Content

Legacy isn't built by what you post today. It's built by what survives tomorrow.

Most marketers are obsessed with the *launch*. The spike of attention. The dopamine rush of likes, comments, or virality. But what separates legacy brands from disposable ones is this: they write, speak, and create through a different lens.

The **Legacy Lens.**

Before you hit publish, ask yourself:

- ***Will this still matter a year from now?***
  Not "Will it get engagement today?" but "Will it still be relevant

when the noise has moved on?" If your content decays with the algorithm, it wasn't legacy… it was just activity.

- *Is this a pattern or a moment?*
  Moments trend. Patterns endure. Patterns are human truths, emotional constants, recurring needs that never expire. The best content ties itself to patterns. That's why people still quote Aristotle, Shakespeare, Drucker, or the Stoics. They weren't writing for the moment. They were writing into the pattern of being human.

- *Does this reinforce who I am — or dilute it?*
  Every piece of communication either compounds your identity or fractures it. Legacy isn't built by trying on a new costume every week. It's built by consistent conviction. The more aligned your message is with your posture, the harder it is to forget.

- *If I disappeared tomorrow, would this be worth rereading?*
  That's the ultimate test. Legacy content is the kind of content people save, revisit, and teach to others long after they're gone. If it doesn't meet that bar, it's not canon. It's clutter.

If the answer is yes, you're not just publishing. **You're planting**, and planting is the most radical act in a disposable world.

Because when everyone else is chasing the flame of virality, you're tending to embers that will still burn ten years from now. When others are addicted to spikes, you're compounding. And when the algorithms forget you, your audience won't because your work gave them language, clarity, and belief they couldn't find anywhere else.

Legacy is not about scale. It's about durability. It's not about how many people hear you once, but rather, how long people carry you with them after.

So, the next time your finger hovers over the publish button, remember: You are not just releasing content. You are building canon. You are planting seeds of identity, resonance, and belief in soil that can outlast you.

That's how you outlive the scroll. That's how you stop playing the content game, and start shaping the culture.

You Are the Signal

Pulling It All Together for a Post-Noise World

You've made it through the signal arc. By now, the pattern is clear: Marketing isn't manipulation. It isn't hacks, scripts, or attention tricks.

It's transmission.
It's coherence.
It's becoming the kind of presence people trust—without ever asking for it.

Over the last chapters, you've learned how to:

- Regulate the nervous system of your audience.
- Collapse resistance without twisting pain.
- Mirror motives and scale relevance without losing intimacy.
- Build messages that compress truth instead of diluting it.
- Align your signal across channels, platforms, and even AI.
- Anchor attention so it lingers instead of spikes and disappears.
- Craft content that doesn't just win a feed—but earns a place in memory.

All of it collapses into one truth:

You are the algorithm.

Your frequency sets the filter.

Your signal decides how you're remembered.

Now, let's look at how real signal builders embody this in the world.

Real-World Signal Builders

1. Andy Frisella — Standards as Signal

Andy doesn't market. He mandates.

His presence transmits discipline, clarity, and no-excuse ownership.

Through 75 Hard, Real AF, and 1st Phorm, his signal is consistency under fire. He doesn't bend to trends — he sharpens through them.

He polarizes around principle and, in doing so, builds a brand that transcends product. It isn't apparel. It's an identity code.

2. Rick Rubin — Silence as Signal

In a world of noise, Rubin makes presence his brand.

He doesn't build hype. He holds space.

His signal isn't what he says — it's how little he needs to say to be felt.

When everyone else is adding, Rubin is subtracting. And the market leans in.

3. Ed Mylett — Emotional Intensity as Proof

Ed doesn't whisper. He transmits.

His words bleed belief — with every syllable a surge of conviction.

His signal is intensity born from embodiment, not performance.

When Ed speaks, people don't just hear him. They borrow his certainty until they can find their own.

4. Joe Rogan — Curiosity as Identity Anchor

Rogan became the world's most powerful media voice not by scripting but by exploring.

His signal is unfiltered curiosity. Freedom to question, contradict, evolve. In that freedom, his audience sees themselves—unbound, unscripted, awake.

Joe doesn't tell you what to think. He creates the room for you to remember how.

What They All Share

- **Coherence**: Their message, tone, posture, and presence match. They aren't playing a role. They *are* the role.

- **Emotional Authority**: They don't argue from expertise. They speak from embodiment. That's what gives their words weight.

- **Signal Density**: Every word, every choice, every product transmits belief. No filler. No fluff. No false notes.

They're not marketing. They're transmitting. They're remembering who they are—and inviting others to do the same.

The New Game

Attention is easy. Belief is rare.

And belief only happens when someone's nervous system says:

"I don't know why… but this feels right."

That is your role now:

- To build a brand that regulates more than it reacts
- To craft content that lasts longer than the feed
- To embody a presence that builds trust without demand

The future won't belong to those who play the content game. It will belong to those who play the **signal game**.

Final Invitation

You're not here to sound clever. You're here to sound true.
You're not here to build funnels. You're here to build faith.
You're not here to compete for noise. You're here to transmit clarity.

Because when the scroll forgets, the signal remains.

You don't need to be the loudest.
You only need to be the clearest.

You are the signal.

Knowing How the Brain Buys Is Power.

But *building a brand that people feel before they think*—that's mastery.

The Neuro Insider Workbook is where everything you've learned becomes embodied. It's not theory. It's transformation in motion.

These pages walk you through the same neuroarchitecting process used to regulate your brand's nervous system, compress belief into signal, and scale coherence across every word, image, and impression you create.

You'll rewire how you think, how you write, and how your audience responds—until conversion feels inevitable. Every exercise deepens identity. Every prompt builds resonance. Every reflection hardens the signal.

Scan the QR code and download your workbook.

Because *information changes what you know.* Implementation changes *who you are.*

THE QUIET POWER THAT MOVES THE WORLD

You've just read a book about marketing. But not the kind they teach in classrooms. Not the kind that clogs feeds or dies in the scroll.

This was marketing as **signal transmission.** As **belief transfer**. As **nervous system resonance**.

You didn't just learn how to write sharper copy or build better funnels. You learned how to **become the message**.

Because that's what the world responds to now:

- Not noise.
- Not hacks.
- Not funnels.

But **frequency.**

You've Stepped into a New Role

You're no longer just a founder, creator, strategist, or brand.

You're a **signal builder**.

And signal builders play a different game. They:

- Regulate more than they react.
- Mirror motives instead of manipulating pain.
- Compress truth into words that don't just inform—but transform.
- Speak from identity, not insecurity.
- Scale trust without ever forcing it.

The tactics matter. But what matters more is the **lens**.

With the right lens, you can see what others miss, hear what others ignore, and name what others feel but haven't yet articulated. That's the mark of someone who doesn't just create noise—but creates meaning.

What Comes Next

This isn't the end of a book. It's the beginning of embodiment.

The world doesn't need more content. It needs more clarity. More resonance. More people who can:

- Speak in neural code.
- Collapse resistance without coercion.
- Build belief that compounds.

The world needs more of you—at **full signal.**

So, go transmit. Not because you're trying to be heard, but because you've become the kind of presence that cannot be ignored.

Let your frequency do the talking.
Let your identity do the marketing.
Let your presence be the conversion event.

This is bigger than business. This is legacy.

Because when you operate at this level, you don't just win markets. You move people. You reshape what they believe is possible—for themselves, for their world, for their future.

And that's the quiet power that moves everything.

You are the signal.

Now go build the future.

BUYER BEHAVIOR CHEAT SHEET

Decode the Nine Hidden Motivators and Convert Without Persuasion

You don't need to manipulate people to make them move. You just need to mirror what already matters to them.

This cheat sheet is your field guide to the **Nine Hidden Motivators**—the deep emotional drivers behind every purchase, action, and "yes."

Use this to:

- Collapse resistance in your messaging.
- Spot motive cues during sales calls.
- Refine offers to match real-world behavior.

Each motivator includes:

- Core desire.
- Emotional tone.
- Buyer cue phrases.
- Hypnotic messaging examples.
- What to *never* say if this is their dominant motive.

Let's dive in.

1. RELIEF

Core desire: "Make the discomfort stop."
Tone: Gentle. Assuring. Release-oriented.
Cue phrases:

- "I just need a break."
- "This has been building for a while."
- "I can't take this much longer."

Use language like:

"You've been carrying this longer than you should."
"Let's release the pressure that's been silently stealing your energy."

Avoid saying:

"You're broken."
(They already feel that—your job is to *lift*, not confirm.)

2. STATUS

Core desire: "I want to be seen as someone better."
Tone: Confident. Elevated. Respectful.
Cue phrases:

- "It's time to level up."
- "I want to be taken seriously."
- "They need to see what I'm capable of."

Use language like:

"This isn't for everyone. It's for those ready to lead."
"Your results should match your reputation."

Avoid saying:

"This works for beginners."
(Status buyers don't want to be grouped with the masses.)

3. CONTROL

Core desire: "I want the wheel back in my hands."
Tone: Steady. Grounded. Reassuring.
Cue phrases:

- "Everything feels chaotic."
- "I need a system that works."
- "I just want to feel on top of things."

Use language like:

"This puts the power back where it belongs—with you."
"Finally, a process that puts you in command."

Avoid saying:

"Let's see what happens."
(That feels like risk—not structure.)

4. ESCAPE

Core desire: "I need out."
Tone: Expansive. Unapologetic. Hopeful.
Cue phrases:

- "I can't keep living like this."
- "I feel stuck."
- "There has to be another way."

Use language like:

"You weren't made to stay trapped in this loop."
"This is the door you didn't know existed."

Avoid saying:

"You'll learn to manage this better."
(They don't want management. They want *out*.)

5. BELONGING

Core desire: "I want to feel seen, connected, and included."
Tone: Warm. Familiar. Tribal.
Cue phrases:

- "It's hard to find people who get it."
- "I miss being part of something."
- "I feel alone in this."

Use language like:

"You're not the only one. You just hadn't found your people yet."
"This is for the ones who've always felt like they think differently."

Avoid saying:

"You're on your own journey."
(Sounds empowering, but reinforces separation.)

6. CERTAINTY

Core desire: "I need to know this will work."
Tone: Direct. Structured. Proven.
Cue phrases:

- "I've tried everything."
- "I need a clear path."
- "I don't want another risk."

Use language like:

"This isn't a theory. It's a framework that's already worked for [X people]."
"You'll know exactly what to do next—and why."

Avoid saying:

"You just have to trust the process."
(That creates tension. Certainty buyers want *clarity*, not faith.)

7. TRANSFORMATION

Core desire: "I want to become someone new."
Tone: Empowering. Expansive. Visionary.
Cue phrases:

- "I know there's more in me."
- "I'm not who I was."
- "It's time to evolve."

Use language like:

"You already know who you were. Let's build who you're becoming."
"You're not here to tweak things. You're here to transcend them."

Avoid saying:

"Small steps can make a difference."
(That's a mismatch. They want the *leap*.)

8. RECOGNITION

Core desire: "I want to be acknowledged."
Tone: Celebratory. Affirming. Public or private, depending on context.
Cue phrases:

- "No one sees how hard I work."
- "It's like I'm invisible."
- "I just want someone to say I did it."

Use language like:

"We don't just teach you. We spotlight you."
"Your work deserves to be seen. Let's make it undeniable."

Avoid saying:

"This isn't about recognition."
(For them, it absolutely is.)

9. MEANING

Core desire: "I want this to matter."
Tone: Deep. Grounded. Purpose-driven.
Cue phrases:

- "I want to do something that matters."
- "What's the point of all this?"
- "There has to be a bigger reason."

Use language like:

"You weren't built to coast. You were built to contribute."
"This is for people who are done chasing and ready to build legacy."

Avoid saying:

"You'll make more money."
(Money is secondary. Mission is everything.)

Final Activation Exercise

Match the Motive, Mirror the Moment

Pick your best-performing offer or piece of content. Ask:

- What's the hidden motivator beneath this?
- Is my current copy matching that motive or muddying it?
- What could I say *instead* that mirrors the buyer's internal emotional logic?

Write a new opening sentence that speaks directly to their **unspoken want.**

Because once you mirror that motive? You don't need pressure.

You've already earned the yes.

THE NEURO INSIDER WORKBOOK: PRACTICAL IMPLEMENTATION GUIDE

Exercises to Reshape Belief, Rewire Behavior, and Build a Brand That Converts on Sight

🜂 PART 1: THE INVISIBLE GAME

Theme: Regulate the nervous system, reframe belief, activate signal awareness

1.1 — Nervous System Brand Audit

"How does your brand *feel* before it speaks?"

- What are the emotions people associate with your presence?
- What would it feel like if someone scrolled past you with no words visible?

Action: Rate your brand's emotional frequency (1–10) for each:

- Safety
- Curiosity
- Certainty

- Resonance

1.2 — Frequency Clarity Map

"Are you creating content that regulates or spikes?"

- What's your natural tone? Calm, intense, chaotic, playful?

- What tone does your *audience* crave?

Action: Identify your most aligned brand frequency and list three types of content that reinforce it.

1.3 — Identity Transmission Statement

"What belief does your presence transfer *without you speaking?*"

Prompt: Fill in:

"When people interact with me, they start to believe that ________."

⚡ PART 2: THE MAP OF MEANING

Theme: Decode behavior, mirror motivation, compress belief

2.1 — Hidden Motivators Exercise

"Why do your buyers really buy?"

Action: Pick three recent sales or client decisions. For each:

- What surface reason did they give?
- Which *hidden motivator* (from Chapter 5) actually drove their action?

2.2 — Mirror the Motive Rewrite

"Rewrite your headline/copy without pain—mirror the motive."

Before/After Exercise:

- Write your current sales copy intro
- Reframe it with identity-based motive language
- Test: Which one *feels safer* and more *resonant*?

2.3 — Compression Drill

"What is the truth you can say in seven words or less?"

Prompt: Write three lines of emotional compression that reflect:

- Your reader's pain.
- Your reader's transformation.
- Your reader's unspoken motive.

PART 3: SIGNAL VS. NOISE

Theme: Scale identity, deepen resonance, protect coherence

3.1 — Signal Density Audit

"Where is your message leaking energy?"

Checklist:

- Is your tone consistent across platforms?
- Are you saying too much to avoid saying *the thing?*
- Do you sound the same at a hundred followers as you would at a hundred thousand?

Action: Highlight one piece of your content. Trim the fluff. Rewrite with compression and coherence.

3.2 — AI Prompt Codex

"Build your own AI training protocol"

Worksheet:

- Define your brand tone in five words.
- Write your go-to emotional metaphor.
- Create three prompt templates that reinforce your signal.
- Codify one belief you want every AI output to reflect.

3.3 — Legacy Filter

"Is this message built to echo or expire?"

Before you publish, ask:

- Will this still matter three years from now?
- Would I reread this if it had someone else's name on it?
- Does this reinforce who I am—or mimic someone else?

⬤ FINAL REFLECTION

Prompt:

"What belief did you enter this book with—and what belief are you leaving with?"

"If your brand became a *nervous system event,* what would it feel like to interact with you?"

THANK YOU FOR READING MY BOOK!

I'd love to connect and stay in touch!

Scan the QR Code:

I appreciate your interest in my book and value your feedback, as it helps me improve future versions. I would appreciate it if you could leave your invaluable review on Amazon.com with your feedback. Thank you!